I'm curious!

The Oxford English Dictionary estimates that there are over 600,000 words in current use.

Compared to other languages, English has a vast vocabulary, with only a few languages having more words to draw from.

However,

Most adult native speakers of the English language, have a range of only 15,000 to 35,000 words.

Why do we restrict our potential by having so few words at our disposal?

Is the key to success to have a larger vocabulary?

Are those with the fewest words at a disadvantage in life?

Use better words
Get better Outcomes!

THE ROAD TO SUCCESS,

IS FULLY PAVED

WITH OBSTACLES

WELL HANDLED.

Jos Frederiks

THIS BOOK IS FOR YOU IF..

You want to change the outcomes you are experiencing right now.

You believe you are not achieving your full potential.

You feel that you are not communicating effectively.

You want to change the culture and success of your company.

You want to communicate better with your partner, family and friends.

What People are saying

Jos is a very charming and friendly individual and an excellent trainer and coach. He builds rapport with people easily and makes them feel comfortable quickly. As an already experienced trainer and coach, Jos brushes up his skills on a yearly basis by attending NLP seminars with Richard Bandler. This not only makes him a highly skilled trainer and coach but also shows that he is passionate about developing himself and other people further. I have learned a lot from Jos and it is always a pleasure to be around him!

Mounia Berrada-Gouzi
Independent multi-linqual event moderator, Emcee & Conference Host. Virtual, In-Person& Hybrid Events!

Jos has been my personal trainer/ Coach since 2010. Working with Jos is a wonderful experience. One of the main reasons that I enjoy about working with his is that he keeps the training varied and always pushes you to a next level – by triggering and influencing the subconscious mind. Therefore the daily sessions are easy, and very pleasant. Each session is different; FUN(!), varied and interesting but also a great opportunity to learn about, and realizing, where I want to be. I would like to recommend Jos as being a great inspirer.

Giel Langeveld
Payment and Telecom industry - operational-, change and delivery management - passionate about high volume operations - Master NLP. Senior Business Delivery Manager.

Jos is an inspiring trainer. Full of passion and expertise, he is genuinely interested in what keeps people busy. He has a wealth of experience and a lot of ready knowledge to provide motivational suggestions. He is a person you would like to have around you.
Walther van Heeswijk
Walther has worked with Jos, but in different teams
Self employed personal coach.

Jos is really amazing, he has such a big knowledge of communication patterns and is one of the few who studies every year with Richard Bandler, founder of NLP. The first time I met him, it felt like we've already known each other for years! He is always willing to share his knowledge with you. Jos is really personable and helps you in both business and personal relationships. I really appreciate his curiosity and it is a pleasure learning and collaborating with him. I really recommend him to everybody who is willing to grow!
Céline

Jos gave a very inspiring and interactive lecture with the theme "Time For A Change" to our Network. Through his life story and insights about burnout and Life in Balance, he managed to trigger us with the question: Is it Time For A Change? It was great to see how quiet the room was and that very beautiful personal stories were shared.

Are you looking for a speaker? Then I can wholeheartedly recommend Jos. He knows how to inspire the audience in a light-hearted and down-to-earth way!
Sanne van Paassen
Mentor for family businesses | Implementation of the new generation | Win business without losing privately | Bestseller Author 'Life, that's top sport' | Speaker | Podcast Host Peak Performance Podcast

I got to know Jos as an enthusiastic, social and driven manager. He is a 'sales animal' through and through. He encourages his employees to get the maximum return from themselves and makes every effort for them to achieve top performance as a team. All this in a casual and positive atmosphere. I have been able to work with Jos for more than two years and have found this to be a very valuable experience!!

Arjen van Eeuwen
CEO at DMCC Group B.V. / Director TQIS B.V.CEO at DMCC Group B.V. / Director TQIS B.V.

When I was told that my job would be eliminated for business reasons, I was put at a crossroads. What now? Should I go straight ahead on the well-known road, which had become a bit too familiar after all these years? Should I turn right, an unknown road but probably going in the same direction? Or should I turn left, onto an untrodden path? I couldn't figure it out. Jos helped me to make the signposts visible at the intersection. His working method was sometimes confrontational, but always inspiring and motivating. I finally turned right.

An unknown road with recognizable landmarks.

Thanks, Jos, for all the insights

Marieke v K.

A major relationship problem. Shocked and no longer functioning normally. The realization that professional help will be needed. I knew I needed it, but at the same time I was also feeling enormous resistance to it.

It made the problem real. The conversations brought a fierce confrontation with the harsh reality. But after the high threshold and the difficult start, the charge was lifted. Thanks to the professionalism of Jos. And thanks to his absolutely unconditional respectful attitude.

I never felt judged. Everyone can learn from that! That's a valuable quality after all. Think about that often. Learned a lot, about myself, about my husband, about us, about relationships and communication in general. And laughed too! Applicable. Even though it doesn't always work out well, we are now very aware of our strengths and weaknesses and can work on them. It has brought good! And trust. In myself. And in us!"
I&T

I will always be grateful to Jos for making me curious about my own use of words. He made me realise that I too have been guilty of talking in automatic and using words without really thinking. If I want to improve my outcomes, I now know what to do. I have no excuse!
Chris Day Filament Publishing

About the Author

Jos Frederiks was born and raised in Eindhoven in the Netherlands to an entrepreneurial family. He started his career as a sales manager in business services and worked at a high level in some of the largest international companies. He quickly learned the value of good communication and how the intelligent use of words can create positive outcomes. He also discovered that he was a natural coach and was often asked by his colleagues for advice and guidance. This helped him develop the art of listening and a curiosity for the way that people use words so carelessly when they talk. As a result he studied and gained qualifications in psychology and Neuro-Linguistic Programming.

In 2005 he took this knowledge and his experience of working with people in the corporate world, and started his own consultancy, VidaSense in the Netherlands.

Jos has become a sought after public speaker and has built a reputation for helping both individuals and companies to change outcomes by communicating better.

According to Jos, "Employers" do not always recognise that the greatest potential within their company is their **people**. Jos's mission is to help them to achieve this potential through better listing and communication skills.

He encourages people to look in the mirror, and ask questions of themselves.

Such as,
- Where do you want to go and what do you really want to achieve today?
- When was the last time that you did something for the first time?
- How do you greet yourself in the mirror in the morning? What words did you use?

I'm just curious. These questions, and many more, are the starting point of every personal conversation or group training."

At VidaSense, Jos is supported by a team of experienced trainers and coaches who work with families, children, schools, individuals from all walks of life and companies of all sizes. Through Life coaching and psychological counselling, he helps people become more motivated, and achieve their full
potential.

THE ART OF COMMUNICATION IS THE LANGUAGE OF LEADERSHIP.

James Humes

Dedication

I want to dedicate this book to my late parents. Without their love and support I would not be here to help you or have written this book. They gave me the wisdom, knowledge, inspiration, dedication, enthusiasm and courage I needed to set out on my life-journey and to succeed. More importantly, they gave me a great love of words and language which set me on the path to my urrent career.

They both helped me in different ways. My Dad was a very positive person and very solution driven. The phrase "This is impossible" simply wasn't in his vocabulary. Everything he saw with his eyes, or even heard about, he could make with his hands. He would always come up with a solution, no matter what the problem.

My Mom, on the other hand, was the thinker and always worked in the background. She was a great listener, a skill she passed on to me, and she never judged. She was smart in many ways but in her early years it was them men who studied whilst the women did the housework (households). She quickly made up for that and learned English when she was 64.

I also want to dedicate this book to my family, Ingrid, Maikel & Jordie. They have always given me the support, time and space to be able to finish this book.

Then to all the passionate listeners, clients, customers, employees, colleagues, friends and beta readers who help me complete it. There are far too many to mention by name!

Many thanks to all of you!

Jos Frederiks

> **THINK TWICE BEFORE YOU SPEAK BECAUSE YOUR WORDS CAN INFLUENCE AND WILL PLANT THE SEED OF EITHER SUCCESS OR FAILURE IN THE MIND OF ANOTHER.**
>
> *Napoleon Hill*

Get in touch!

Everyday life is full of challenges for us all. Sometimes, talking things through with a sympathetic and experienced pair of ears can be a help. It is so difficult to find anyone to listen these days.

VidaSense is a psychologist's practice in Eindhoven & Helmond for children, youth and adults. Our team consists of remedial educationalists, psychologists and hypnotherapists. We have the experience, qualifications and background to offer the best possible support.

At VidaSense we believe that every human being is unique. One size does not fit all. This is why our greatest talent is listening carefully to your experiences, story-lines and needs.

There are many ways we can support you. Just call us for a chat without any obligation.

To connect with Jos Frederiks for public speaking enquiries or about his services as a Life Coach, a Trainer or as a Business Psychologist, see over the page.

Contact Details

Call +31 85 060 9596
E: info@josfrederiks.com
www.josfrederiks.com

VidaSense Website
www.vidasense.nl

For VidaSense, call:
Tel: +31 85 060 9596

No matter what people tell you, words and ideas can change the world.

Robin Williams

IMPRISONED BY WORDS

Jos Frederiks

Published by
Authoritize
14, Croydon Road, Beddington
Croydon, Surrey CR0 4PA
www.authoritize.co.uk
+44 (0)20 8688 2598
hello@authoritize.co.uk
Authoritize is a division of Filament Publishing Ltd

© Jos Frederiks 2024

ISBN 978-1-915465-53-5
All rights reserved

The right of Jos Frederiks to be identified as the author of this work has been asserted by him in accordance with the Designs and Copyrights Act 1988 Section 77

No portion of the book may be copied in any way without the prior written permission of the publisher.

Printed in the UK and Europe

Table of Contents

	Foreword - Raymond Keene OBE	19
1.	What have you got to say for yourself?	25
2.	Life without Words	29
3.	Healed by Words	45
4.	My Career	53
5.	VidaSense - A new start	71
6.	Words and Outcomes	87
7.	The Two Briefcases	93
8.	People Pleasers	99
9.	Playing with Words	113
10.	Becoming a great communicator	121
11.	Words to keep us safe in the sky	129
12.	Words at home	137
13.	Talking to children and teenagers	145
14.	Corporate Culture	157
15.	Job interviews	185
16.	Communicating as a manager	193
17.	Chosing your words	201
	Appendix	211

"I KNOW THAT
YOU BELIEVE YOU
UNDERSTAND
WHAT YOU THINK I SAID,
BUT I'M NOT SURE
YOU REALIZE THAT
WHAT YOU HEARD IS NOT
WHAT I MEANT."
EH?

Robert McCloskey

Foreword

BY RAYMOND KEENE OBE

INTERNATIONAL CHESS GRANDMASTER

William Shakespeare can be credited with many achievements, not least, in my opinion, with writing the key texts which actually created English national and linguistic identity.

Shakespeare's play *Henry VIII* brings to a close the mighty history cycle commencing with *Edward III*, now generally regarded as, at least partly, a Shakespeare original, and one of the very few which specifically mentions chess: "And bid the lords hold on their play at chess, For we will walk and meditate alone." Scene 3 in the Royal Shakespeare Company edition.

The cycle continues with *Richard II, Henry IV Parts One and Two, Henry V, Henry VI Parts One, Two and Three, and Richard III*. It is my opinion that this huge dramatic cycle, essentially one long play, represents the true English national epic in a way that Beowulf (too early in our national lifeline) and Paradise Lost (too Latinate for most readers, though a treat for those who like their English poetry in a Latin word order) do not.

If I am correct, then the Shakespeare histories together create our epic poem of national identity, on a par with Homer's Iliad and Odyssey, Virgil's Aeneid, Dante's Divine Comedy, the Welsh Mabinogion, Finland's Kalevala, Portugal's Lusiads and for the Jewish people, the epic story of the Hebrew Bible, or Old Testament.

In the course of his plays and poetry Shakespeare deployed a vocabulary of around 35,000 words, a global record , apart from James Joyce in Finnegan's Wake , who operated with a staggering vocabulary of over 64,000 . However, many of these were one off inventions , never since revived and incomprehensible to the multitude, not so much caviar to the general as gibberish to almost everyone, apart from Joycean scholars ensconced in their most adamantine of ivory towers.

In contrast, the most literate of English users tend to operate within a maximum of 15,000 words, with the average being closer to 3000/5000.

Vocabulary liberates thinking and creativity , according to the author of this startling new book, which equates freedom of expression with breadth of thinking and outreach of communication potential.

Indeed, in an increasingly restrictive communicative environment , ruled by emojis, icons, abbreviations , with would be aspirations to eloquence, arbitrarily truncated to a prescribed maximum of characters, verbal grunting rather than efflorescence , the full expression of cerebration is now widely regarded as an evil to be avoided at best , or ignored at worst. Brevity may be the soul of wit, but that does not necessarily imply that expression at full length is anathema to our little grey cells.

That the author should have fastened onto the English language as the prime vehicle for his lucubrations, is all the more remarkable , given that he is a Dutchman born and bred, a nation with its own rich literary tradition, which includes Vondel, Multa Tuli and Harry Mulisch.

There is no doubt that Jos has a passion for words and a fascination with how they are used and the impact they can have.

But it is in his skill at listening that enables him to make a big difference in helping others.

In my own writing, which includes 207 published books on chess, mind sports, the nature of genius, poetry, art, biography and quantum physics, I consciously seek to give certain underused words their place in the sun, lest they be ignored, forgotten and ultimately retired. Such worthies include ultracrepidarianism (pontification on a subject, about which one knows nothing); oenophile (wine lover) and Porpentine (Shakespearean for porcupine). I draw the line, though, at James Joyce's fabrication nntrovarrhounawnskawntoohoohoordenenthurnuk.

This 100-letter monster appears on the first page of Finnegan's Wake. The word is a phantasmagoric concoction, which rightly belongs in the ephemeral cabinet of curiosities, from which it so infelicitously escaped.

Meanwhile, do enjoy this guided tour through the foothills and peaks of self expression which will help you both to impress and influence your fellow practitioners of the English language, the fortunate and uniquely combined linguistic heir of that opulent triumvirate of cultural roots, Grecian, Latinate and Germanic.

Ray Keene

Raymond Keene OBE

Raymond D Keene OBE is an international chess grandmaster, former British and EU champion, author of 207 published books, with translations into 16 languages.

He is fluent in French and German, can struggle in Dutch, Russian, Spanish and Latin and has published over 12,000 regular columns in such publications as : The Times (London) The Spectator, The Article, The International Herald Tribune, The Gulf News, The Australian (Sydney) The Daily Yomiuri (Tokyo) The British Chess Magazine and The Gibraltar Magazine.

He has read Beowulf and Sir Gawain and the Green Knight in the original old and Middle English, translated Goethe's Faust from German and has attempted the first page of both Kant's Kritik Der Reinen Vernunft and James Joyce's Finnegan's Wake.

WORDS ARE SINGULARLY
THE MOST POWERFUL FORCE
AVAILABLE TO HUMANITY.
WE CAN CHOOSE TO USE
THIS FORCE CONSTRUCTIVELY
WITH WORDS
OF ENCOURAGEMENT,
OR DESTRUCTIVELY
USING WORDS OF DESPAIR.
WORDS HAVE ENERGY AND
POWER WITH THE ABILITY TO
HELP, TO HEAL, TO HINDER, TO
HURT, TO HARM,
TO HUMILIATE
AND TO HUMBLE.

Yehuda Berg

Chapter One

WHAT HAVE YOU GOT TO SAY FOR YOURSELF?

No matter where you currently are in life, whether you are in a good place or a challenging one, it is your choice of words that have put you there. That might appear to be a big statement, but it is a fact that people do judge us by what comes out of our mouths. What else have they got to go on? We can talk ourselves into trouble, it's easy to do so. But... we can also talk ourselves out of it. It depends on how intelligently we use our words.

Wherever we are in life right now, it is our words that have put us there. Just think for a moment where you might have been right now, if you had a better vocabulary? Has your use of words held you back?

BANISH THE WORDS
'I CAN'T' FROM
YOUR VOCABULARY.
REMEMBER: IF 'CAN'T'
EQUALS 'WON'T',
'CAN' EQUALS 'WILL.'

Phyllis George

Have people put a label on you based on the way you speak? The good news is that this can change! And you are the pilot!

As infants, we learn about the impact that our first words have on our parents. Whether it is "Mama" or "Dada" the warmth, gratitude, love and appreciation we receive from them from our saying our first words, teaches us how powerful they are. In our early school days, when we were given the chance to speak in class, it marked us out as someone who can use words effectively. It identified us as a future communicator. We learned that the right words, well-spoken gave us power.

Without a doubt, words are the most powerful force in the universe. Words are what cause people to act both for good and also for bad.

HEALTH IS NOT VALUED TILL SICKNESS COMES.

Thomas Fuller

Chapter Two

LIFE WITHOUT WORDS

I have often wondered that, if we did not have any vocabulary, what sort of thoughts would we have? If we were unable to describe the way we think with words, what would our thoughts look like? Thoughts are the internal dialogue we have with ourselves to solve problems and to make decisions. Most of the time, our thoughts are silent. We rarely think out loud but are we missing something by keeping them to ourselves?

As an author there is something that I have noticed. When I am being interviewed, and I have to respond to a spoken question, that is unexpected and unprepared for, I am often surprised by the quality of my answer. Where did that come from? Questions seem to trigger access to deeper and hidden memories in the brain which come to the surface in a fluent and unexpected way, to contribute to my answer..

The brain has to respond instantly to a spoken question and will often surprise us with its answer. We often think "Where did that come from?"

When we speak an answer, we very often say things that we might not otherwise have thought about.

In 1948 the poet W H Auden wrote, **"Don't ask me what I think until I have heard what I am going to say"**. Quite profound!

It seems that the brain does a deeper search when it is asked a random question than if it that question was just read. Very often we surprise ourselves!

It is the spontaneity of an unexpected question that seems to trigger this. I call this **Subconscious Verbalisation.** You may well indeed learn something new when listening to yourself! This only happens when you are asked a question!

I believe that Self-Talk is also a very powerful tool in helping us to think better and perform better. At the start of each day we have an open book of possibilities. Our day can be whatever we choose. Good or bad. Amazing or challenging. The first word we speak at the start of the day defines our attitude at that moment and will trigger what happens next. **"You are the pilot!"** Don't leave your day to chance, choose your first words with care!

Personally, first thing in the morning, when I get up and walk past the bathroom mirror, I look at myself and smile. Well, why wouldn't I? Starting the day with a smile is a good start. If you verbalise something positive at the same time, you will get double the benefit.

The thing about self-talk is that it has to be just that. You actually need to verbalise your words, not just think them. Spoken words have a stronger effect on the brain than just thoughts. Of course, people around you might be concerned to see you talking to yourself, so you might not want to practice this on the bus on your way to work!

What is the most powerful self-talk? It is when we challenge ourselves with a question, out loud. Then speak the answer. Your brain is now an active participant in your conversation.

There is another aspect of self-talk and that is, it can help demolish barriers to sharing your deepest thoughts.

Picture this. A young lady of 13 years old came to my practice together with her mother. She didn't want to be there, but her mum insisted that she should come.

She was facing a hard time letting go of her emotions and she wouldn't talk about it. Her mum knew that it was blocking her in many ways and was convinced that professional help would make a difference.

They both came to my office even though she knew it would not make any difference. We greeted each other and took our places in the room. After a little introduction and the small talk, I asked her what she was here for.

"I am not going to talk," she said. "I don't have any problems to talk about."

I ignored what she said and we spoke generally for ten minutes, but I was not able to break through the barrier she had erected and get her to engage with me. This frustrated her mother.

She was very smartly dressed. Everything matched perfectly and I complemented her on it. She started to smile and talked about her interest in fashion in a relaxed way. However, when I changed the subject back to her, once again she blocked the conversation.

Then I had an idea. I took out some hand puppets from the Muppet Show. I asked her which one she wanted and she chose Kermit. She also picked puppets for me and her mother.

From that moment, she started to speak in Kermit's voice and took on his character. We started to improvise a dialogue between us all. This broke down her barriers and she was able to talk freely about herself. This form of Self-Talk, talking through a third party, can help to make a difficult conversation easier, when you are talking for somebody else rather than about yourself.

We kept using the puppets for communication, and it worked very well.

This became our preferred method of communication.

After several sessions she came up herself with the idea of talking straight with me and the puppets had been an icebreaker.

Thoughts can become trapped if we are unable to turn them into words. Words, when spoken can demonstrate how we feel and share that with others. Our words will determine how they then react to us.

In all circumstances, your choice of words determines what happens next. Choose them well – from the first word you speak in the morning to the last word you speak before you go to sleep.

Self-Talk is valuable. If you don't have Kermit to talk to, do what thousands of people do, and have a conversation with their dog or cat. They are incredibly good listeners!

So, what kind of day are you going to <u>choose</u> to have today? There is no luck involved, it is all in your choice of attitude, as expressed in your words! When you broadcast those words to those around you, you are telling them how to react to you.

Will today be...

- Just another day at the office,
- Exhausting!
- Disorganised
- Overwhelming
- Insufficient time to do everything
- Stuck in the wrong habits
- Directionless
- Without purpose?
- Aggravating?

OR will today be...

- Exciting
- Full of opportunity
- Purposeful
- Satisfying
- Educational
- Amusing
- Calming
- Loving
- Caring

The choice is yours!

Don't let anyone else decide the sort of day you are going to have!

I often ask colleagues in my office about their use of Self-Talk. Interestingly, when trying to come up with a solution to a problem, many of them use a form of Self-Talk and have an internal two-way conversation within themselves to discover the answers. They whisper the conversation so as not to disturb those around them, but it still counts. Have you ever tried asking yourself an actual question out loud? You might be surprised at the results!

There are two types of Self-Talk, Positive and Negative. Actually we need both! To arrive at the correct solution to a problem, we need to examine both positive and negative solutions and then compare the potential outcomes of both.

We can have a healthy discussion with ourselves through self-talk that can be more productive that just thinking about an issue on one dimension. Verbalising this discussion give us more options to consider and better solutions as a result.

This way you are constantly challenging your thoughts and not settling for second best. There is always a solution to everything but it might take an internal discussion with yourself to identify it.

Language Barriers

Relationships are very personal and special. When things go wrong, the pain that can be caused is almost unbearable. I was working with a beautiful couple who came from two different cultures. The guy came from a country where they use language in a strong way to express themselves and the girl was totally the opposite. She was a petite, soft-spoken lady and looked very beautiful. They were deeply in love, but one year later, something had gone wrong, so they came to see me.

When we met she was in tears. She told me that when they both met he would bring her flowers and speak beautiful words to her. In recent months though, he had become rude and uncaring to her. She told me that having differences in the past was not a problem as they had been able to talk things through. But now he is swearing and cursing. He was no longer acting like the man she fell in love with. All of a sudden that original magic was gone. She was devastated.

When I spoke to the man, he agreed that in his culture, there was a lot of swearing, and for him, that was normal. He understood that this was not the case in her country, and the way she was brought up. He went on to highlight that neither of them spoke the language of the other. The only language they had in common was English which was what they had to use. However, their vocabulary in English was limited, which made it difficult for them to communicate as clearly as they would like. The guy, all of a sudden, discovered that he had a lack of words. It was their lack of words that was stopping them from communicating in a proper understandable way.

This was not made any easier by the fact that he was self-employed and things were difficult for him. Imagine this, he was arriving home stressed at the end of the day, and she was looking forward to see him again but she was not looking forward to the way he spoke to her and the words he used which was negative and complaining.

They start avoiding several topics. She was in a completely different industry, so they had little in common with their work. She liked to share information about her day and wanted to know how his day went. They had drifted apart because they lacked the right words to bring them together. They were imprisoned by their lack of words!

When two people need to make use of one language, in this case English, some things are more difficult to talk about than would be the case in your native tongue. Things can be easily misinterpreted when you are struggling to use the right words. Imagine this in a relationship?

The couple asked me what they should do next. I asked him what made him stop using precious and beautiful words to his wife? In the beginning he knew how to use them and he did use them. He told me that his work demanded a lot from him and that he got frustrated easily. He knew that it was not good to project this onto his wife but he just couldn't help it, he said. He made her cry easily and they were just drifting apart.

I also asked them how much time they took each week to have a proper conversation and to tell each other what they liked and what they want to achieve in their relationship. This was not something they were currently doing. It was just when things went wrong, that they started shouting at each other which led to fights.

I reminded them that they both really wanted the same thing and the simple things they could be doing is to demonstrate their love and respect for each other.

Sometimes all it takes is time and the right words to bring people back together.

The first assignment that I gave them was to schedule some good, quality time for each other. They could pick and choose what they wanted to talk about.

Another assignment that I gave them was to use as many different new positive words in a conversation as they could and to talk to each other about what they liked.

Another wonderful tool to use is asking questions, lots of questions! Too many people don't ask questions at all. What message does that convey? That you are not interested in finding out the answers! I assume that you do want to know the needs of your partner? When I ask questions to people about what they really need, they find it difficult to put their answer into words. This is the same for both partners! To be good communicators you have to practice!

Spend more quality time with your loved ones. Demonstrate how you feel about them by being interested in their thoughts and feelings.

At the moment of writing, I can tell you that the couple managed to bring back the spark that they needed. It started with taking time for each other and with the caring use of words.

Discovering Words for the First Time

When we start out in life, everything we learn we do so by listening. We have no language. We cannot speak or ask questions. We look to the people responsible from bringing us into the world. Our parents!

Watching a baby learning how to speak for the first time is beautiful to watch. So also, is the competition between parents as to whether the baby's first words are 'Momma', or 'Dada'.

A new baby is a blank canvass just waiting to be pained on. It has no language, no judgements, no preconceptions, no memory of a past. Its total focus is its parents and trying to understand what they are communicating to them. Their listening skills are probably the most acute they will ever be in their lives.

Since these early days, learning to make sense of sounds and understanding the meaning of words takes our full concentration, As we mature, you would think that our listening skills would improve, but sadly I don't think that is true. Distractions get in the way and we develop the art of Selective Hearing.

Selective hearing

Selective Hearing is when we don't focus on the detail of the conversations around us, but instead we listen out for Keywords related to the things that our subconscious minds are interested in. We filter our everything else.

This mode of listening only works if you have multiple conversations happening around you. Keywords just jump out of the cacophony around you and enter your consciousness. This does not work if you are having a direct conversation with one person which requires your complete focus. In these circumstances, if you were concentrating on other things, it would be obvious - and very rude! If we are to be effective as communicators, our ability to listen is essential. It is worth, therefore, understanding the types of listening so we know what is the most appropriate for any given situation.

Active Listening

This is the highest form of listening. We are fully engaged and totally focussed on the person talking. Not only are we listening to their choice of words, and the intention of what they are saying, but we are also aware of their body language, expressions, gestures and intonation, and to discover other clues as to what their words actually mean. With active listening, we are at our most attentive and receptive. It is always stimulating to converse with an active listener.

I REMIND MYSELF EVERY MORNING: NOTHING I SAY THIS DAY WILL TEACH ME ANYTHING. SO IF I'M GOING TO LEARN, I MUST DO IT BY LISTENING.

Larry King

It is flattering to speak to someone who demonstrates their interest in what you are saying. These days it is a rarity!

Reflective Listening

This is the natural progression from Active Listening. It is where you think back on what you have heard and look at how relevant it is to your current situation. Not everything can be instantly understood. Often there are layers of meaning that were not immediately obvious. You need time to reflect in order to appreciate what was said.

Informative or Critical Listening

Similar to Reflective Listening, Critical Listening is when you listen with a a specific outcome in mind. It does not mean that you are listening to be critical but rather than you are focussed on evaluating or analysing a specific topic.

Biased Listening

This is where you apply a filer onto what you are hearing and blot out anything which appears not to be relevant to the information you are seeking. You measure a conversation by how it supports your own views, judgements and prejudices. You are likely to reject any opinion that clashes with your own.

Closed or Defensive Listening

Technically, this isn't listening at all as you are not really interested in what the other person is saying. You are only interested in when they stop talking, so that you can get your next point across. Rather like a bad salesman or a politician!

LISTENING EMPATHETICALLY

This is where your focus is entirely on the person you are talking in a caring way being sensitive to their needs. This way of listening beings comfort, support and healing and demonstrates our care for the other person.

The one thing that so many people lack is the opportunity to share their worries and concerns with somebody who is prepared to listen. For anyone in need of comfort and support, talking to someone who is prepared to listen is a great gift.

This type of listening is used in therapy sessions and creates a feeling of safety.

Listening is a great art and needs to be practiced. It takes awareness and discipline for you to avoid interrupting and cutting across them when they are talking.

The benefit to the listener is that you are tapping into somebody else's vocabulary. You may well discover they are using words that might be new to you. Listen and Learn!

Healed by Words

I discovered how powerful words can be when I was 19. From an early age I had very bad asthma. So bad that I had constant difficulty with breathing. When I was nine and again when I was eleven, I nearly died as a result. I was spending half my time in the hospital. Asthma was ruining and controlling my life.

I was getting so frustrated with my health that I had no choice but to do something about it. The doctors didn't seem to be able to do any more than to treat the symptoms, give me medicines and provide me with oxygen. This was not helping the underlying cause, whatever that was! There had to be something. I just needed to think and have a serious conversation with myself. I have always believed that if you need to think something through, the best place to do it is in the car. (at least it works for me)

So I asked my Mom for the car keys. "Where are you going?" she asked. "I am just going to drive," I said "I need time to think." Today is going to be my last day suffering from Asthma. "That's impossible she said". "I said, please leave me alone and let me do my thing".

MUSIC HAS HEALING POWER. IT HAS THE ABILITY TO TAKE PEOPLE OUT OF THEMSELVES FOR A FEW HOURS.

Sir Elton John

So I got into the car, a Peugeot 404, a very nice drive. I took with me a small cassette player with some soothing piano music to play.

I play piano myself and it has always helped me feel instantly relaxed. I remember that the first track I played on my journey was "Sleepy Shores". This soothing piece is played every night on BBC radio just before the shipping forecast. With this playing in my ears, I set out, with no particular destination in mind.

I found myself on the road to Antwerp. I looked at myself in the rear-view mirror and said to myself, "This is the last day that I put up with asthma. I am fed up with not being able to breathe properly, not being able to play sport and not being able to join social activities. "I want to become healthy and feel better." I said to myself, This became my mantra as I drove.

So, using the rhythm of the music to help me breath more regularly, I started to take longer and longer breaths (making sure also that the intervals between breaths was also longer). I started talking positive words to convince myself that I could get better. Initially, my breaths were not enough for me to say what I wanted, and I kept coughing. This was discouraging, and nothing was changing for the better. As I progressed along the journey, I found I was able to increase the intervals between breaths and to speak for longer with one breath. Things were starting to change just a little bit.

Every breath we take, every step we make, can be filled with peace, joy and serenity.

Thich Nhat Hanh

I arrived at Antwerp and was starting to feel a little better, but I knew I still had much more progress to make. So, I took the road to Brussels, and kept practicing my positive self-talk. Something magical happened between Antwerp and Brussels. I noticed that, all of a sudden, I could catch more oxygen with one breath. My breathing was noticeably better. Three and a half hours later, I arrived back home to find my mom waiting for me, she was in a state of shock and worried about me. "Where have you been?" she shouted.

I said to her, "Look at me! What do you see? Do you notice anything different about me?"
"No," she said, initially but then it dawned on her
"You are not asthmatic!" I said "Yes, it's reduced by at least 80%.!" "That is not possible" she said!"
I explained to he her what I had done and how, by controlling my breathing together with the music and talking positive words to myself, my asthma has improved dramatically. Having seen me struggling for breath for the last nineteen years and nearly dying twice as a result, she couldn't believe it. "I am determined that it won't come back," I told her, and to this day it has not returned!

WISDOM IS THE REWARD YOU GET FOR A LIFETIME OF LISTENING WHEN YOU'D HAVE PREFERRED TO TALK.

Doug Larson

Of course, I am not a doctor, and I am not saying that this is a wonder cure. All I am saying is that this was a very real experience for me and I believe that the use of positive words contributed to making a real change to my health. I have never forgotten that experience. To me, that was the spark that gave me an interest in the power of words and, later on, even the idea for this book, "Imprisoned by Words", but in my case, I do believe that words actually saved my life.

Much is talked about positive reinforcement and self-hypnosis but at that time I knew nothing about either of those concepts. All I knew was that I was determined to make a dramatic change to my health, and to convince my body to do so. Today, I see the power of words making changes in the lives of the many people I work with. I see them using words differently themselves, and changing their outcome as a result. I see words, chosen with care, helping people to make closer connections, and avoiding conflicts. As a result, I firmly believe that if you indeed do change your choice of words, you will be amazed at the new doors that open for you and the new opportunities that will arise.

Before any conversation, think of the outcome you would like to happen. Then choose the words that will help to make it happen. Test it yourself! It works!

Listening is a magnetic and strange thing, a creative force. The friends who listen to us are the ones we move toward. When we are listened to, it creates us, makes us unfold and expand.

Karl A. Menninger

Chapter Four

MY CAREER

Looking back at my life, I seem to have been very fortunate that in every job that I have had, I discovered something new about the power of words, how they can work for you. And also how they can work against you if you do not choose them wisely!

As I left school and started moving into the world of work, I was fortunate to be accepted on a work placement programme organised by VW, Audi and Porsche. I was hired by one of their dealerships and this became my first job. I loved cars so this seemed like a great place to start.

Watching my colleagues in the different departments, I could see the importance of clear and precise communication. At one end of the scale was the service department which dealt with customers and arranged for repairs. At the other end of the scale were the salespeople who were focused on developing a rapport with the customers and helping them make a buying decision. Two very different styles of communication.

One day a young man of about 19 or 20 came into the showroom dressed very scruffily with sneakers and jeans. He asked for a test drive in an Audi all-road Quattro, a very expensive and beautiful car.

IMPRISONED BY WORDS

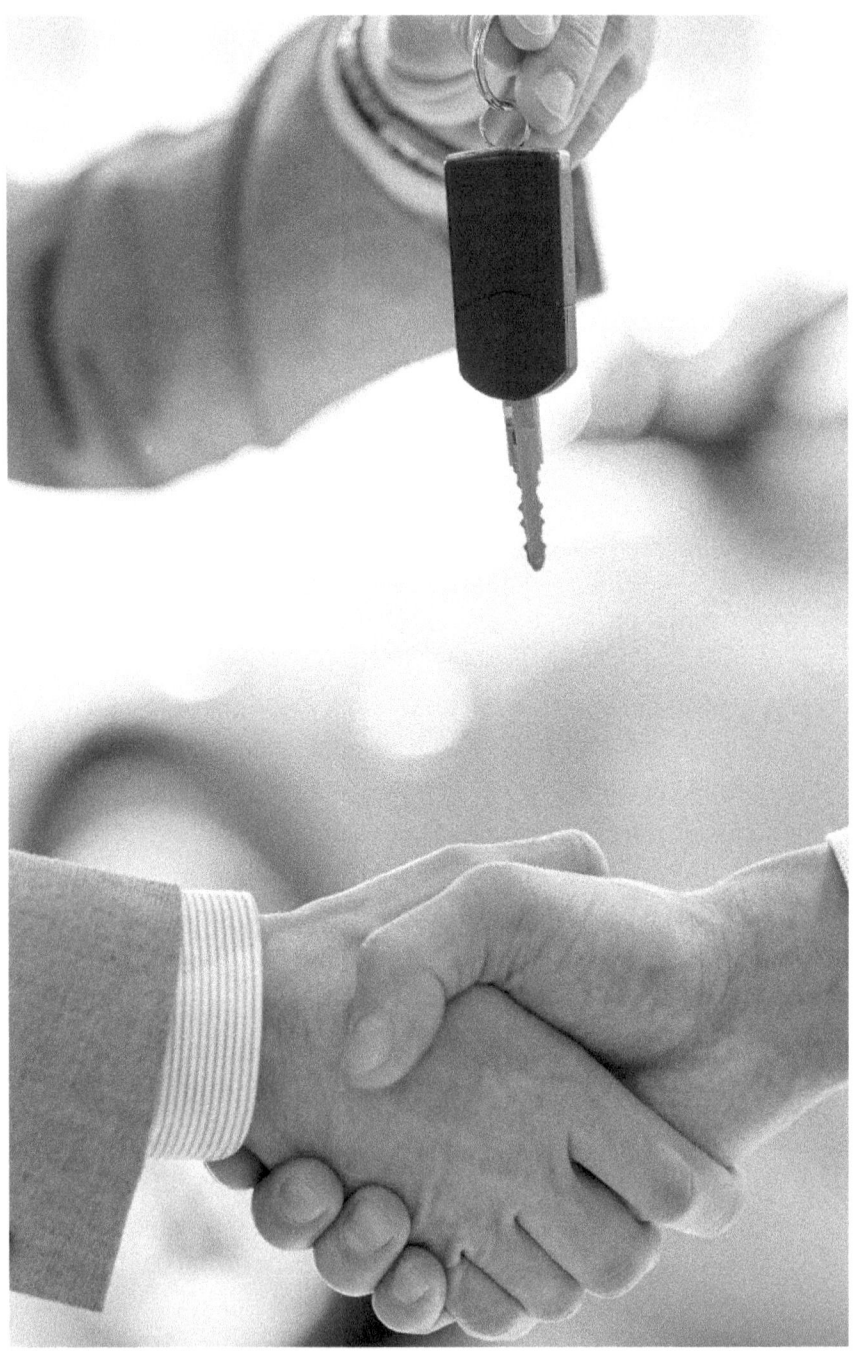

To be honest, I didn't know what to think in the beginning, but my dad always taught me to treat every person gently, no matter how they are dressed. I told him that we didn't have the model in stock at the time but that we could get one for a test ride. I spoke to my sales manager who duly arranged for one to be brought onto the forecourt.

A week or so later the customer returned and was delighted that we had found the car he wanted. We went for his test drive – or thrill ride as it turned out! He certainly knew how to drive fast! After a scary ten minutes, I had to say to him, "If you want to drive at that rate, it's okay with me but you will need to buy the car!" "OK I will," he said "does it come in red?" "Yes it does," I said "Let's do the paperwork." And we did. In just thirty-five minutes, I had made my first sale with the company for around €95,000. A great to start to my career in sales.

Once we got back, I asked him why he bought the car so quickly." He said, "I went to a lots of dealers including the big names. Nobody took me seriously because I came in as a young kid in jeans and sneakers. They just ignored me. Nobody would give me a test drive with their most expensive car. However, you just asked me the right questions, made me comfortable and gave me the test drive that I wanted. I had promised myself that, if I go to a dealership and I'm treated right, I'm going to buy the car from them. And that's how it happened."

Selling is essentially a transfer of feelings.

Zig Ziglar

I learned a huge lesson then about pre-judging. I learned that it was not about how people look but what they have to say, that mattered. I had to ask questions in order to get answers. From that experience, I also learned that I had to be a better listener. Those two qualities have changed my life.

I went on to sell many more cars and had fun doing so. I stayed there about a year but then I wanted to broaden my experience, so I moved on to a truck supplier. It was a large company with premises in a number of counties. They were into heavy goods vehicles and buses. They also had a marine division and other specialist divisions. My clients now included coach builders.

The culture of this company was very different to the first company I worked for. Being so much larger, they had a big infrastructure and were very systems-orientated. I was still in sales but I became interested in the full range of products they had for sale.

I discovered that, in one division, they converted the cabins on international trucks to install a sleeping bunk for the driver. In another division they produced a high-quality brass windows that were used in luxury boats. I immediately saw the potential of linking them up and using them for the sleeping compartments of trucks.

I spoke to my manager who was dismissive of the idea of selling them to another division.

Too many people today know the price of everything and the value of nothing.

Ann Landers

"These things will be too expensive for them" he said. I said, "Yes. So what? Well, leave that up to me. I don't sell on pricing." "So you say!" and he left me to it.

So I took a sample hatch with me and went to a company I knew in the southern part of the Netherlands. I knew the buyer there was a very tough negotiator and always wanted the biggest discount. Before I met him, I spoke to some of his mechanics. They looked at the sample and were very impressed. They confirmed that it perfectly fitted their production process and they suggest that I showed it to the buyer. This was my intention all along!

So I met the buyer, knowing that he would want to negotiate on price. But I wasn't going to play his game. "I have something interesting to show you" I said when I met him and showed him the sample. "I believe it will perfectly fit into your manufacturing process. This is a hatch. This is something which is used in the boat industry, to go on the top of a sleeper bunk. And I think you could use it in your process, and on the side little window of a truck's cabin"

"I know that this stuff is expensive, what's the price of it?" I said, "I know you are the best estimator in the company so I have a totally different question for you. Tell me what do you think how much the price may be? What would you like to pay for it?"

When he had finished I said "Don't show me yet. I will write a number on a piece of paper and I will see how close we are."

NOTHING IN THIS WORLD CAN TAKE THE PLACE OF PERSISTENCE. TALENT WILL NOT: NOTHING IS MORE COMMON THAN UNSUCCESSFUL MEN WITH TALENT. GENIUS WILL NOT; UNREWARDED GENIUS IS ALMOST A PROVERB. EDUCATION WILL NOT: THE WORLD IS FULL OF EDUCATED DERELICTS. PERSISTENCE AND DETERMINATION ALONE ARE OMNIPOTENT.

Calvin Coolidge

So I put down my price and turned over my piece of paper. He did the same. I then invited him to reveal his. It was €600. "Is that your final price?" I asked him. "Hmm, maybe €650", he said. I then turned over my piece of paper. My price was €500. "I must have made a mistake" he said "But you are the best estimator in the company. Surely not?" "Alright, he said, give me a sample to try." So we did.

A week later, I returned to see him. First I spoke again to his mechanics and learnt from them that the hatch was perfect and in fact, took a shorter time to install. Armed with this, I returned to visit the buyer.

I went inside and I asked them "Well, now you have used it, do you like the product?" "Yes" he replied but we got to talk about the price." I said, "Yes I agree" I said "because I offered it to you far too cheaply." He ignored me and said "You will have to do something with the price." "Certainly I can increase it for you with pleasure." "But I need a discount!" he said. "You are the best estimator in the company. You took your time to make your calculations and you came up with a price of €650. My calculation was a price of €500. You already have a big discount, which you calculated yourself! The price is €500, take it or leave it!" After a little complaining, he took it at €500. Not only that, but in the following year he ordered many hundreds more, making this a very significant sale.

> **Strive not to be a success, but rather to be of value.**
>
> *Albert Einstein*

After we made the sale he laughed and complimented me on the sales process which was the first time he had been sold to in that way.

If I had used the traditional sales process based on ever-reducing discounts, we would probably never have closed the sale with this margin. We succeeded because of an innovative way of using words and putting the emphasis on value.

When I returned to my office, I found that the vice president wanted to see me. Rather than compliment me on the large profit was made on the order, instead he wanted to know "What the hell are you doing with the products that we sell for the boating industry?" I said, "You don't like what I'm doing?" He said, "Yeah, I love it, but what the hell are you doing with that product?" I said, "I sell it." He said, "Yeah, but you never give any discounts." I said, "You don't like it?" "Yeah, of course I liked that." I said, "In that case you can give me a raise as I am selling so much!" He had no answer to that but to say yes.

The point of this story is to demonstrate that the way we use words determines the outcomes we have. Increase your vocabulary and only good things will happen. Certainly, the vice-president and I had very different conversations in the future.

> You can have everything in life you want, if you will just help other people get what they want.
>
> *Zig Ziglar*

I had been in the truck supplying market for some years and one of my clients suggested to me that it would be a good career move to move up to a larger company in the world of leasing products. I set my sights on the biggest company of its type in Europe. He had a connection there and made an introduction. I made one phone call and landed a new job with an increased salary and perks. I ended up being with them for nine years.

It was a big cultural change working in a such massive organisation. There was a hierarchy of communication and you could only speak to people in your department. Corporate Culture and the way communication works in an organisation is fascinating. There are formal lines of communication that you have to respect. You cannot speak to just anyone, you need to go through a structure in order to get to the person you want to speak to. I was given incredible freedom to cut across those lines. I worked my way up through the structure and was finally responsible for corporate markets in the Netherlands.

A big responsibility and I was good at what I was doing, but nothing is forever.

Some time later, a colleague I knew was leaving and told me he was moving into the growing telecoms market with a company called Talkline, which specialised in mobile phones, SIM cards and data. It sounded interesting. Some six months after that he called me out of the blue to find out how I was.

It's not what you achieve, it's what you overcome. That's what defines your career.

Carlton Fisk

Knowing it was not like him to make social calls, I said to him "Cut the crap, why are you really phoning me?" "Well,", he said, "there is a position available which is perfect for you, and I'd like to come to Utrecht to find out more". I told him that I knew nothing about mobile phones and data. "That's not what we are looking for. I'm looking for people who know how to handle people. You are a people manager, you know what to do with people. That's what I need." So I went to Utrecht!

I arrived there quite late at 7 pm and went to the office where the receptionist welcomed me by name, she did this with great enthusiasm. I apologised to her that I had arrived so late in the evening. She laughed, "You're not late" she said "the entire team is here waiting for you and they are really looking forward to seeing you!" Wow! I thought. What a welcome! I then met all the directors who had prepared an extensive and detailed presentation for me about the business. I remember there were sixty-five slides, but I can only tell you what was on the first and the last one! Sometimes, if you want to convey an important message, less can be more.

I started in the field as a junior account manager to learn the business. When you are starting a journey, you have to start at the beginning, not half-way down the road. I had a lot of learning to do about the company structure, company culture, systems, products, processes, people, their roles and responsibilities. I climbed the ladder, just like everyone else, and was soon promoted to Key Account manager.

In the journey of an entrepreneur, the most important thing is self-belief and the ability to convert that belief into reality.

Mukesh Ambani

I then joined the management team with responsibility for the corporate market. I was given plenty of support by my director, Philip, and the opportunity to have learning opportunities – or make mistakes to put it another way!

He was generous in sharing his knowledge and helping me to grow. I used the opportunity to increase my knowledge of psychology and learn about the way people think in the University. The company encouraged me in this. I started to learn more about the power of words and the science of communication which I found fascinating.

I was with Talkline for seven and a half years and saw the company through various restructures. When I started with them, there were thirty-five employees. When I left, there were 925. I loved my time with them and loved what that time had taught me. I had seen at first hand how a business can thrive when it puts its people first – not it's customers! In reality, if you look after your people, they will do the same to your customers.

Finally we were sold to another company, and not the one I would have chosen in the first place! This was also a great journey to learn more about structure, hierarchy and the way business is played inside a company. After two reorganisations, I got fired at the third one together with another 130 dear colleagues.

The time was now right for me to move on and to start my own business to share what I now knew. VidaSense was born.

Chapter Five

A New Start

Setting up VidaSense was a huge change for me. Working as part of a huge business shields you from many of the challenges of life. You don't have to worry about money, as it comes in at regular intervals every month. There is a well-defined structure that everyone complies with and everyone knows what is expected of them. Of course each company is money driven and the bottom line is always the bottom line.

I was making a difference, I was working with people who I liked but I suppose I was in bit of a comfort zone. I had survived two big reorganisations, but the third one was too dramatic to get through. One hundred and thirty people were let go, including myself. It was not a pleasant experience!

It was time to take stock and take charge of my own future. I had sent years trusting the various companies I had worked for, to look after me. But now my future was up to me and nobody else!

One big advantage that I had was the circle of friends and fellow professionals who I had met and worked with on the years. It was they who encouraged me to set up a business, doing what I had been doing before but for a wider client

base of small businesses and individuals. VidaSense was an immediate success and I found that the listening skills I had developed, made it easy to understand the needs of my new clients.

I also quickly learnt that, when you do not have the security of a big organisation behind you, all of the things you have become used to you, such as holidays, perks expenses and company cards, had vanished overnight. The buck now stopped with me! As did the bills!

I was already used to listening to people and helping them to gain clarity. Now it was my business to do so., I became fascinated in the words my clients were using and how, in many cases, what they were saying was not really what they meant to say.

I would often use my clipboard to write down what they just said and read back to them the actual words they had spoken, and often, they were often shocked and surprised to hear what they just said; when you speak automatically, you don't hear what you say. You only remember what you meant – which may not be what was heard!

Starting up a new business was a huge opportunity. There was so much I wanted to do to help others. Through my experience, I knew that if I could help people to be better at listening to what others were actually saying and for them to be far more aware of the words they were using, their outcome could be greatly improved.

IMPRISONED BY WORDS

I remember a situation where words helped to cure a bad phobia.

I was speaking to a lady whose world was getting smaller by the day. She was frightened to go out, frightened of crowds. Even when she was forced to go out to collect the kids from school, she tried to make herself small and invisible. She was also telling herself that she was not able to do it. Her language and her thoughts were limited. Her body was full of negativity. Even going to the shops was a frightening experience. Her way of thinking was badly limiting her life.

She asked me 'Where is this fear coming from?' I said to her, "I don't know, but I think that I could help you find the answer. Would you like me to help?"

"This has been going on for so long that I cannot see me getting rid of it, but I am willing to try!" So she booked a consultation.

There are actually only a small number of basic fears that people have. There is the fear of falling – not from a height, but of falling over. Another is fear of loud, unexpected noises – even yelling and slamming doors can be frightening to some.
So, I asked her "How do you rate that your fear?"

She answered "I know it is irrational. I know there is nothing hurting me. I know it is all in my mind but I don't know what to do!"

REAL MAGIC IN RELATIONSHIPS MEANS AN ABSENCE OF JUDGMENT OF OTHERS.

Wayne Dyer

I looked at her and asked the next question.

"Imagine you knew what to do, would you do it?"
She looked around and said, "I suppose so."
"Hmmm interesting answer, so that wasn't a direct yes then?"

"Let's visualise what this fear looks like. Close your eyes and tell me what you see"

"Its really big." I asked her for permission to hold her hand and she agreed.

"Reach out and touch your fear" She extended her hand wide in front of her.

"You have taken the fear out of your head and you are holding it in your hands. Do you want to get rid of it?
"I really do" she said

"Let's make it smaller" She brought her hands slightly closer together.

"Even smaller!" She moved her hand even closer.

"Do you really want to get rid of it?"

"Yes!" she said

In my early professional years I was asking the question: How can I treat, or cure, or change this person? Now I would phrase the question in this way: How can I provide a relationship which this person may use for his own personal growth?

Carl Rogers

"OK, here we go! Five, Four, Three, Two, One!" and I brought her two hands together in a clap.

"Your fear is now scrunched up on your hand. Now throw it away over your shoulder" She did so.

"So you have thrown your fear away. It is gone. You had the power all along! How do you feel?

"Actually, a lot better" she said. We repeated this five times. Finally I said

"So now put the picture of your fear in front you. What does it look like?"

"I can't find it any more"

"Do you want me to find it for you"

"No thank you!"

This sounds very simple to people when I tell them. As a matter of fact it can be that simple.

A week after she came back and the first thing I asked her was "Is it still gone?" She tensed up, "No, not completely. I think it will be impossible for me to lose it completely" she said.

There are so many great things in life; why dwell on negativity?

Zendaya

I asked her how many times she had practised positive reinforcement since our first session. She told me "None at all!

"You told me at our first meeting that you did not expect to cure yourself in just one session. This would be too good to be true"

"That's right"

"If you really want to get rid of your limiting beliefs and lift this weight from your shoulders, will you undertake to do daily exercises at home in front of your mirror?"

She agreed. We did the session again and I gave her some positive language to use at her home sessions

A week later she came back to see me with a big smile on her face.

She told me that she practised it daily in front of the mirror. In the beginning, it felt very awkward. She looked at herself in the mirror and started to think about how great it would feel to bring her kids to school feeling relaxed. She could now visualize herself doing this, which before, she couldn't. She got into the habit of changing her language patterns.

She told me that, after weeks of practising, she now felt completely released. "I never could have thought that I would be able to make such a difference in my life with just language!" A great result!

THINKING WILL NOT OVERCOME FEAR BUT ACTION WILL.

W. Clement Stone

It is not just words that can produce powerful results, it is also when you turn them into questions.

I was out shopping in a grocery store when I saw a beautiful sight. A young girl of around three years old was sitting on the floor beside her mother. The mother was engrossed in a magazine that she had picked up from the display. The young child did the same. The difference was that the child was holding the magazine upside down! She looked for a moment and then realised that things didn't look right, so she turned it the right way up and continued reading. She looked very cute as she was copying her mother. A BIG smile came on her face and she continued reading and looking at the pictures.

Just then her mother looked down and saw what she was doing. Instead of encouraging her, the mother shouted at her loudly for everyone to hear. "What are you doing? Put it back, put it back!" I was taken aback at such a harsh reaction when the poor child was doing exactly what her mother had been doing. Not surprisingly, the child was devastated and started crying uncontrollably.

This was in the middle of the shop on a busy Saturday afternoon, and everyone turned to see what the matter was. But the mother continued to shout.

"Put it back and don't touch it!"

WHAT IS A FEAR OF LIVING? IT'S BEING PERMANENTLY AFRAID OF DYING. IT IS NOT DOING WHAT YOU CAME HERE TO DO, OUT OF TIMIDITY AND SPINELESSNESS.

THE ANTIDOTE IS TO TAKE FULL RESPONSIBILITY FOR YOURSELF - FOR THE TIME YOU TAKE UP AND THE SPACE YOU OCCUPY. IF YOU DON'T KNOW WHAT YOU'RE HERE TO DO, THEN JUST DO SOME GOOD.

Maya Angelou

I looked at the mother and we made eye contact. She looked back aggressively. What? she shouted at me. What are you looking at? I held my gaze and lowered my voice.

I was just looking at you and your little girl and I wondered if there was a specific reason why you were speaking to her in the way you did? She looked surprised. "What?" she shouted again. What are you talking about?

I remained calm with my voice lowered. Okay. I will repeat the question. What reason did you have to speak with your daughter in the way that you did? Is there a specific reason why you would ask your daughter to put the magazines back in the way you did?

At that moment, you could have heard a pin drop. Everyone was looking at her and waiting to hear what she would say. And something magical happened. The child stopped crying and looked at me. The mother paused but said nothing. She just picked her daughter up and left the shop.

One of the guys in the queue beside me said, Whoa! That was an interesting question you asked!" I looked at him and replied I was just curious about what was going on in her brain. She wasn't behaving well towards her daughter, and she knew it. It wasn't my place to tell her that, but I just wanted to make her think and realise what she was doing.

We don't need to judge a person, you never know what might have happened one hour before she entered the shop. Being curious will open someone's brain and they can do with it what they want.

It takes but one positive thought when given a chance to survive and thrive to overpower an entire army of negative thoughts.

Robert H. Schuller

Chapter Six

Word and Outcomes

By now, my business was well-established and growing. I was attracting a cross-section of clients from individuals, couples, children, business owners, managers and organisations. All of them use words in different ways to achieve outcomes.

I quickly realised that, if I was going to challenge clients for the way they were talking, I had to make sure that I gave a good example myself. What I insisted on was that, in every conversation, all the parties concerned were 'Present'. I don't necessarily mean 'occupying the same physical space' but rather that they were not being distracted and were focused on our conversation.

In reality, when we listen to somebody we are only giving them half of our attention. The other half of our attention is trying to work out what we are going to say next. I now make sure that people are listening to me by asking them questions. That forces them to give me their full attention.

But there are some people who are only able to speak and unable to listen.

I once knew a president of a big company who had a robust way of communicating with the staff.

**WHATEVER WORDS
WE UTTER SHOULD
BE CHOSEN WITH CARE
FOR PEOPLE WILL
HEAR THEM AND
BE INFLUENCED BY THEM
FOR GOOD OR ILL.**

Buddha

There was very little subtlety in the way he spoke. If he wanted something to be done, he simply gave a command. However, this style may not have gone down too well at home, because he was now divorced and onto his second wife.

The truth was that he had difficulty in communicating not just at home but with his staff as well. Without the ability to choose his words well, he just barked commands.

He was telling me about his twelve-year-old daughter who was at elementary school. He has high expectations of her and wanted her to behave more like an adult. I just told her, he said. You should work harder at school and give it your best shot. You need to get into gear and do your utmost best. Then things will turn out great!

I looked at him and asked, well is she doing her utmost best? Is she getting into gear? He shook his head. No she isn't - and I don't think she even understood my question.

I looked at him and said I am curious to know what she is thinking? What questions did you ask her? He replied, Well, that was the question. I replied, Was it a question, or was it a command? He hesitated, well now you put it that way, I suppose it was a command. I don't find it easy to choose the right words at the right moment.

I felt sorry for him so I asked him this question. How much time do you spend preparing for a conversation with your daughter or even with one of your employees?

BE NICE TO YOUR CHILDREN. AFTER ALL, THEY ARE GOING TO CHOOSE YOUR NURSING HOME.

Steven Wright

Do you think about the words you are going to say or about the outcome you want from that conversation? Do you have a plan?

If you are telling yourself that this conversation is going to be difficult, then your brain will prove you were right.

Think how it will be for your daughter, or indeed anyone else you need to talk to. Are you making it easy for them? Or are you putting up barriers? I could see he was thinking. Let me make a suggestion. Start by asking a question. By doing so, you are demonstrating that you are interested in her and what she thinks. It also means that this will be a conversation, not a lecture.

Demonstrate that you are curious about what she thinks. "Curious?" he asked. Yes, and always start by using her name. It makes it far more personal. When you are curious about what people think, it opens up a different part of their brain. She is not being defensive about being spoken to, instead she is being treated like an adult, and entering into a meaningful conversation. Ask her opinion about what she thinks. How she would tackle a situation and what outcomes she would like.

By making a deliberate choice to use words that are inviting, encouraging, inspiring, or supportive, you will completely change the nature of a conversation with somebody and leave them feeling good. What difference do you think that would make to those around you, and how they felt about you? A good conversation is a two way street. You need to listen as well as talk.

IMPRISONED BY WORDS ───────────────────────────

Chapter Seven

THE 'TWO BRIEFCASE' RULE

For many of us, we exist as two people. One part of us is the husband, wife, boy or girlfriend living at home. We are surrounded by 'home' or relationship problems and decisions. When we go to work, we become a different person. We act differently, and speak differently. Think of it as having two briefcases. One briefcase is full of what is happening at home. The other is full of our work worries.

The problem arises when we take our home briefcase to work - and spend the day worrying about everything inside it. Then, to make matter worse, when we get home, we take out our work briefcase and spend the evening worrying about all the things we needed to do at work. The result is that we are not truly 'present' either at work or at home. This affects our ability to focus and to communicate effectively.

The only answer is to take the work briefcase to work and leave the home briefcase at home. Being truly 'present' wherever we are, is vital for good communication - both in listening as well as talking.

> **THINK TWICE BEFORE YOU SPEAK, BECAUSE YOUR WORDS AND INFLUENCE WILL PLANT THE SEED OF EITHER SUCCESS OR FAILURE IN THE MIND OF ANOTHER.**
>
> *Napoleon Hill*

The biggest obstacle to good communication is when we don't listen fully to the person talking to us. and only half hear what they said.

Probably, we were too busy thinking about our reply to have fully heard the question. This is not surprising because, from the earliest age, we have only been taught how to talk and not how to listen.

Why do we have two ears and only one mouth? Because we need to listen twice as much as to speak. It is a skill that I needed to learn as well - and it took practice!

Communication has to be two-way - or it is a monologue

It is always the responsibility of the communicator to confirm that the message they are giving is clearly heard and understood. In the same way, a waiter would always repeat back to you the order you have just placed. They would always check that you are happy with your meal.

The art of effective communication has changed dramatically over recent years. Before the internet came along if we wanted to send a message, the only option was to write a letter. That simple act of writing a word, instead of talking made each word more considered. Originally there were multiple mail deliveries in a day.

Deep in conversation!

It was possible to post a letter in the morning and receive a reply by the evening. Those were the days!

Today the traditional art of writing with a pen is dying. People now use their thumbs to create a stream of lower-case words on their smart-phone without any attempt at punctuation. Few can even read their own writing. Words have become mechanical and not the well-crafted art they used to be. And that is not all!

The Millennial generation hardly even talks! Put two people next to each other and they would far prefer to be texting each other instead of having a real conversation. In fact, in the USA it has now become possible to run an entire country just by using twitter! But there is an upside to everything.

If you are a lover of well-crafted words then you will have the one skill necessary to attract into your world the right people and to create the opportunities you need to succeed.

Good words are all you need to open doors! If you can communicate, you will have a big advantage over the many that can't.

The best way to find yourself is to lose yourself in the service of others.

Mahatma Gandhi

Chapter Eight

PEOPLE PLEASERS

Inbuilt into our DNA is the need to please people. When we are nice to people, they are nice to us. A perfect situation. The first law of the hospitality industry is to give people what they want – and they will come back.

In return for being nice, we get appreciation, recognition or sometimes just a smile. But is it enough? It must be a fundamental need because it also applies to animals Cats will purr and dogs will roll over for a tummy rub. Every living creature loves positive attention. It is natural for us all to want to say Yes.

Yes is an empowering word that opens the door for something good to happen.

IMPRISONED BY WORDS ———————————————

Dogs never lie about how they feel

JOS FREDERIKS

In 2008 there was an American romantic comedy film starring Jim Carrey and co-starring Zooey Deschanel called "Yes Man". Jim Carrey goes to a positive development seminar which promoted the idea of saying Yes to everything. He takes the decision to adopt the idea and starts to say Yes to everything that comes his way. As you can imagine, what followed was unexpected and not what he imagined.

The other side of that is that many people try and avoid saying No to people because it might upset them. They will look for imaginative ways to avoid saying No and end up talking in circles. A bit like a politician who doesn't want to answer a question. By not communicating clearly, and speaking in a confusing way, we can cause upset, annoyance, a lack or clarity and a loss of respect. Always say what you mean, and mean what you say!

In the 1960s there was a television quiz show starring Des O'Connor called 'Take Your Pick'. In it was 'The Yes/No Game'. Contestants had to endure 60 seconds of questions

I USED TO THINK THAT THE WORST THING IN LIFE WAS TO END UP ALONE. IT'S NOT. THE WORST THING IN LIFE IS TO END UP WITH PEOPLE WHO MAKE YOU FEEL ALONE.

Robin Williams

but could not use the word 'Yes' or 'No' in their answers. If they did, a gong would sound and they were disqualified.. The results were hilarious. It demonstrated how much we want to say yes even when we try not to!

For example, if someone told you not to think about your left ear, what is the first thing you do? That's right, you start thinking about your left ear. Because the word "not" is something we mentally ignore, so the question we actually hear is. "Think about your left ear. "

Take some time for yourself to think about being a people pleaser. Are you or aren't you? What does it bring you? Do you gain any advantage by using it? I am curious what will happen in a relationship when people start to please each other on a great level. What you give is what you get!

TOO OFTEN WE UNDERESTIMATE THE POWER OF A TOUCH, A SMILE, A KIND WORD, A LISTENING EAR, AN HONEST COMPLIMENT, OR THE SMALLEST ACT OF CARING, ALL OF WHICH HAVE THE POTENTIAL TO TURN A LIFE AROUND.

Leo Buscaglia

Have you ever listened to yourself?

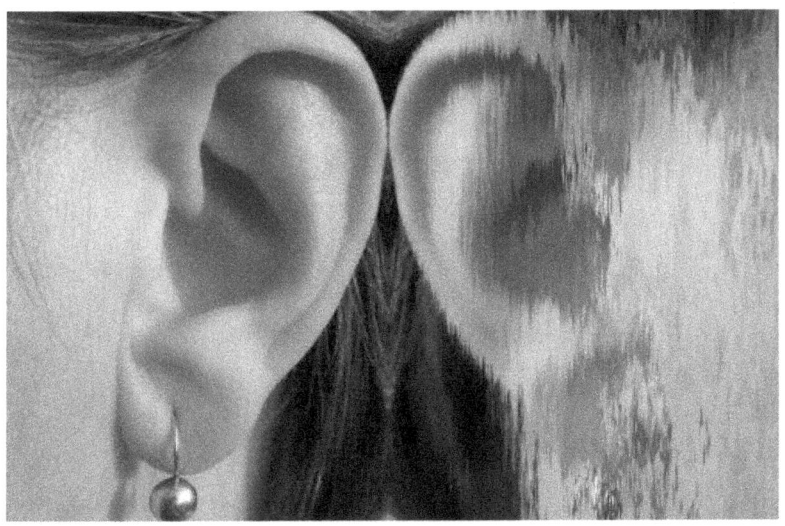

No, Really Listened!

For the last seventeen years, I have made a point of listening to conversations very carefully and I am amazed at what people say, when they actually meant something very different.

When I repeat their actual words back to and ask them if that is what they meant, very often, it is not.

Listening carefully is an art, and one which needs to be practiced and developed.

IMPRISONED BY WORDS ───────────────

AN INTELLECTUAL IS A MAN WHO TAKES MORE WORDS THAN NECESSARY TO TELL MORE THAN HE KNOWS.

Dwight D. Eisenhower

As a communications professional and coach, I have probably listened to over 18,000 conversations. It is true to say that the outcomes of all of them could have been vastly improved if the people concerned talked on purpose, not by accident.

One of the best ways of doing this is by asking questions. You need to think to answer a question, which is no bad thing in a conversation.

Over the years as an employee, then a manager, to a director and then as a coach, mentor and trainer, I must have taken part in many thousands of separate conversations. I came to the conclusion that few people are aware of precisely what they are saying. I have often proved that on stage and in a workshop, by writing down on a flip chart, word for word what somebody said. When we then analyse the words that were used, they have realised that the message they were conveying was not what they meant. It is as if our default setting is to just say what comes into our heads without a second thought.

It is also the case that our words reflect our mind-set and our attitude. Everything we say betrays who we are. If you are negative, or suspicious, or angry.

Our choice of words will make our inner thoughts as clear as day. With our thoughts we make our world. However, I would add to that because thoughts on their own cannot create action.

> **We sometimes encounter people, even perfect strangers, who begin to interest us at first sight, somehow suddenly, all at once, before a word has been spoken.**
>
> *Fyodor Dostoevsky*

It is the words we say that conveys those thoughts, and causes things to happen.

So here is a question. Have you ever actually listened to yourself? Have you ever used a digital recorder to capture your words and then play them back? It is worth doing!

Listen, not just to your words, but also the overall message you are conveying. Are you saying what you meant to say? What do you think the person you were speaking to, thought you said?

THE THINGS WE FAIL TO SAY

We need to perfect the art of communicating in the moment, and thinking in the present. What is that one word? A word of appreciation? A word of support? A word of recognition? What could we have said to make that brief conversation more powerful and memorable? What word could make their day?

A word of consolation; a word of support; a word of congratulations; a word of understanding. Being interested in them, even for a moment, is precious to them.

I have been mindful of the number of people who live alone and hardly speak a word to anyone all day. We are living in a increasingly lonely world. We must be mindful about the positive impact of a random word to a stranger.

IMPRISONED BY WORDS

Crack the Code   №1

A B C D E F G H I J K L M N O P Q R S T U V W X Y Z

1	2	3	4	5	6	7	8	9	10	11	12	13
14	15	16	17	18	19	20	21	22	23	24	25	26

ANSWER: 1=R, 2=G, 3=S, 4=P, 5=A, 6=K, 7=L, 8=I, 9=N, 10=B, 11=E, 12=V, 13=U, 14=X, 15=C, 16=T, 17=D, 18=M, 19=H, 20=V, 21=O, 22=F, 23=Z, 24=O, 25=J, 26=W.

108

The gift of giving somebody the opportunity to share their words is a wonderful thing to do. You have two ears and one mouth. Use them in that proportion. The other real advantage of listening with generosity is that you never know what nugget of gold you might receive and what you might learn.

> **I REMIND MYSELF EVERY MORNING: NOTHING I SAY THIS DAY WILL TEACH ME ANYTHING. SO IF I'M GOING TO LEARN, I MUST DO IT BY LISTENING.**
>
> **LARRY KING**

WORD SEARCH PUZZLE
COUNTRIES OF THE WORLD

```
U C A M B E N I V P H V E N I A L P U B
R D E N M A R K N A G E Z O C D V A N O
I A G O D T O V A N O N T D I A E R D L
O N Y R N A J Q L E C E R H N D N G A I
B A O W A I T C A M A Z E N I M E A R A
U J P A I N O T S E M U K R K O W E D L
L Y E G Y P T A U Y E E B U W E N O N A
G D N A L A E Z W E N L W R N P E R A M
A S O D G E R M A N Y A N O N A B E L U
R C O N E M Q U G A I L O I K R A N E G
I A R A Z A G D U T C B D A Y A Q R C A
A M E L R A U E A S E O A L R G E F I E
S B M I R K A N L Z O L C A G U S A N T
Z O A A M N Y O E Y N I A M Y A T I A A
T D C H U R V R S G E V I E T Y A N L V
A I K T U E V W A R A I S T A R N E S O
N A M O N Y E A N Y B A I A K A O M T D
R Q R I A Z G Y S K H L N U D E I R A L
E G A N E T H I O P I A U G U M Y A N O
N A T S I N A H G F A W T H A I T N C M
```

ICELAND
PARAGUAY
CAMBODIA
CANADA
NICARAGUA
ESTONIA
KUWAIT
GERMANY
YEMEN
GUATEMALA
SLOVENIA
ETHIOPIA
THAILAND
KYRGYZSTAN
LEBANON

NORWAY
CAMEROON
EGYPT
NEW ZEALAND
JORDAN
AFGHANISTAN
BULGARIA
ARMENIA
VENEZUELA
IRAQ
DENMARK
UKRAINE
BOLIVIA
MOLDOVA
TUNISIA

Chapter Nine

PLAYING WITH WORDS

I feel ready for anything if I have eaten well first thing.! Our brains are the same. If you give them a diet of interesting, inspiring, creative and stimulating words, they will perk up and become more creative.

Imagine working or living in an environment where words are used only when absolutely necessary. Where people communicate to the person beside them by text not talk. How can the brain be stimulated in those circumstances?

When you use words in a fun and playful way, people just love to talk to you. Words are the only thing we probably have in common with each other. Don't talk just to communicate - use your words to stimulate, challenge, spark a witty reply. Words are far too much fun to waste on feeble conversations.

I was working with a client once and sat taking notes as she spoke. In fact I was writing down exactly what she was saying, word for word. When she had finished I asked her if I could check that I had heard what she said correctly and I then read back to her the exact words she had used. She was more than a little surprised.

It is the supreme art of the teacher to awaken joy in creative expression and knowledge.

Albert Einstein

"Is that what I actually said?". "It was." I replied. "Well hearing it back like that, I feel awkward.

It didn't come across as I would have liked it to." "Would you like to do something about it?" I asked "Absolutely! But I don't know how." she said. "OK," I said "but suppose if you did know, what would you do?"

And then an unexpected thing happened. It was as if her brain had been switched on. She started to talk, but this time she was really in flow. Instead of talking in a disjointed manner, she was suddenly on a creative roll. When she stopped I asked her. "Well how did that feel?" "It was amazing!" she said "I don't know what happened to my brain, but it felt really good."

I explained that when you ask 85% of people on the planet a question, they will probably answer "I don't know." Even if they know the answer. It is less effort to say nothing than to speak.

But if you then challenge them by saying "I know you don't know, but if you did know, what would be the answer?", they suddenly become fluent and their creativity is unlocked.

I have also noticed, that people can be shy and need to be coaxed into a conversation.

It is easy to say "I don't know" but once you get past that, there is often no stopping them.

A SINGLE CONVERSATION ACROSS THE TABLE WITH A WISE MAN IS BETTER THAN TEN YEARS MERE STUDY OF BOOKS.

Henry Wadsworth Longfellow

I remember a careers teacher who used this technique. When interviewing pupils to find out about their future career choice, most of them would mumble. "I don't know." However, when she then asked "But if you did know, what do you want to do?" she would get a very specific answer, "I want to be a chef!"

THE POWER OF QUESTIONS

There is no doubt that asking the right questions is the best way to cut through the lazy habit of talking without engaging the brain. If you were to analyse much of your conversation throughout the day, most of the things we say are shallow and more like an auto-responder than a conversation.

However, a good question is impossible to ignore. It demands an answer, and more importantly, it requires us to think - not just respond.

The more curiosity to display , the more interest you have in the person you are talking to, the great likelihood there will be in having a deep connection with them.

Most people can go for days, or even weeks, without being challenged to have a direct and meaningful conversation.

To be a good leader, you have to be a good communicator. As a leader, you have to communicate your intent every chance you get, and if you fail to do that, you will pay the consequences.

William H. McRaven

They spend their time giving bland, responses to insincere questions from people who are not actually interested in their answer. They were just being polite.

As a result, we get out of practice with our conversational skills. It is only when you make a deliberate choice to properly engage with somebody does the real magic happen. And you do this by demonstrating your genuine interest in them and your curiosity in what they think or feel. It is good questions that are the key to unlocking our real thoughts.

I have spent a lifetime listening to people speaking and reflecting their words back to them. Almost every time, people are shocked by what they hear. Did I really say that? They ask. Indeed they did.

However, the greater clarity I help them to discover and the more that they carefully think before they speak, there is one thing I can't help with. These are the words that are left unsaid. The things we fail to say.

There is a moment for every word. An instance in time where only that word will do and none other. There is a moment of need when somebody pauses and waits for you to say something. Will you miss that moment?

IN A HIERARCHY, EVERY EMPLOYEE TENDS TO RISE TO HIS LEVEL OF INCOMPETENCE.

Laurence J. Peter

BECOMING A GREAT COMMUNICATOR

Becoming a great communicator doesn't happen overnight. It takes practice. You need to perfect your listening skills as well as your speaking skills. As part of this process you will make mistakes. It is only natural.

Use every conversation or meeting as an opportunity to improve. Replay it in your mind and be objective with yourself as to how you did. For example, did that conversion achieve its objectives? Were you sure of the outcomes you wanted to achieve before you started it? Did you say something which upset or annoyed the other person? Did you listen carefully to what they were saying or were you thinking more about what you were going to say next?

Were you speaking in a negative way or were you inspirational and uplifting?

The way we use our words is crucial. Was it in a limited way of speaking or very positive?

What I discovered after so many conversations with people is that they start to create a sentence in their mind while the other person is still talking.

> I THINK WE ALL
> HAVE EMPATHY.
> WE MAY NOT HAVE ENOUGH
> COURAGE TO DISPLAY IT.
>
> *— Maya Angelou*

As a result, they don't really hear what the other person just said. Your response to them is to what you thought they said, rather than what was in their mind. Communication is full of challenges if you are not totally in that moment.

This can be more acute when speaking to a boss or superior.

In a company, this is something called 'fear of hierarchy.' You cannot imagine how much people suffer from this fear. Often, it builds up over a period of years and then all of a sudden, they find themselves in the middle of a conversation that they feared the most. It is never going to go well when all of that pressure is released.

Some of us do feel uncomfortable when there is a silence in the middle of a conversation. You need to respect the style of the person you are talking to. Maybe they need a moment to process what you just said before responding. Sometimes a tiny pause can be very helpful in getting clarity before speaking. You will get to understand the way different people prefer to communicate and adjust your style to suit their needs. Don't forget that this works both ways!

What kind of style do you use towards your employees? Is it always the same or do you adjust to the different kinds of people in your company? How much awareness is there of communication at all? What kind of style do YOU prefer and does the receiver knows this?

SOCIETY EXISTS ONLY AS A MENTAL CONCEPT; IN THE REAL WORLD THERE ARE ONLY INDIVIDUALS.

When you start to analyse your style, you quickly see that there is much more to good communication than just exchanging just a couple of words.

I will never forget the story at a popular bar on the rooftop in the centre of Eindhoven. One of the things which made it popular was the way that the waiting staff took a real interest in their customers and making them feel welcome and at ease.

The barmen was only concerned with getting the drinks served quickly and resented the seemingly wasted time the waitresses to in talking to their customers. He expressed his annoyance by being annoyed and irritated with them. He simply didn't understand that building rapport and a good connection encourages customers to spend more and recommend that place to others. Their style of communication was highly appropriate even if he couldn't see it. It is these soft communication skills that can make all the difference to a business and the customer experience.

I hear many employers say, "my employees are the most valuable assets in my company." In so many organisations, I wish that this was true!

We spend more time at work than almost anywhere else. The chances we are there because we need the income, rather than for any other reason. However, the time we spend in the office doesn't have to be unpleasant, it really is up to you and the person you want to be seen as.

Kindness in words creates confidence. Kindness in thinking creates profoundness. Kindness in giving creates love.

Lao Tzu

If you come over as rude, disinterested, aggressive, devious, negative, or simply not nice to be around, then this is what will be reflected back on.

They say that everyone lights up a room. Some as they arrive, some as they leave. Which one are you? Have you noticed that some people simply drain you of energy, whereas other inspire and motivate you, just by being around.

An office environment is a complex interaction of diverse individuals, each with their own agendas, values, egos and focus. You are in a zoo and you need to find out which animals bite, which demand to be fed and which roll over to get their tummies rubbed (metaphorically speaking!) You need to act intelligently to survive and thrive and you will need to your senses about you. In any hostile environment you need to listen, and listen hard. The words people use will tell you a lot about them. Of course, these words will be supplemented by their body language, and their tone of voice. All of them clues as to the actual meaning of what is being said. At the same time, they are all evaluating you by everything you do and say. Your choice of words is critical to survival.

Speaking of Body Language one thing to remember is that that it never lies! Experts believe that our words only make up some 7% of the message we convey. 55% is our body language (gestures, posture and facial expressions) and 38% is the tone of our voice.

There is no point in working on choosing the right words if our body and our tone of voice are saying something very different.

A good exercise is to watch other people talking. Compare the words they are using, and their tone of voice with their gestures and their body language. Are they congruent? Are they both saying the same thing? Sometimes not!

Our children know us better than anyone else. They study us constantly for clues as to what we mean, what we are feeling and what is on our mind. We need to do the same, we need to communicate with them directly and honestly.

Don't judge them. That will instantly shut down all communication. Learn to be a good listener and somebody who is easy to talk to. Don't put up barriers and take a position. Just be there for them and let them make their own mistakes, just as you did. It is the only way to learn.

LISTEN WITH THE INTENT TO UNDERSTAND, NOT THE INTENT TO REPLY.

STEPHEN COVEY

JOS FREDERIKS

Chapter Eleven

WORDS TO KEEP US SAFE IN THE SKY

Before then invention of cockpit voice recorders and Blackbox flight recorders, it was incredibly difficult to piece together what went wrong in the event of an accident in the air. However, with this technology, accident investigators can now fully understand what actually happened leading up to a crash. They made an important discovery.

The International Radiotelephony Spelling Alphabet, commonly known as the NATO phonetic alphabet, is the most widely used set of clear code words for communicating the letters of the Roman alphabet.

Alfa,

Bravo,

Charlie,

Delta,

Echo,

Foxtrot,

Golf,

Hotel,

India,

Juliett,

Kilo,

Lima,

Mike,

Papa,

Quebec,

Romeo,

Sierra,

Tango,

Uniform,

Victor,

Whiskey,

X-ray,

Yankee,

Zulu

The biggest contributory factor in a plane crash we not mechanical failure, nor was it a failure of aircraft handling skills or technical knowledge.

The biggest problem was communication between the crew. It was WORDS that were the cause, or the lack of them. Inadequate communications between crew members and other parties could lead to a loss of situational awareness, a breakdown in teamwork in the aircraft, and, ultimately, to a wrong decision or series of decisions which result in a serious incident or a fatal accident.

NASA was brought in to come up with a solution. After analysing hours of cockpit recordings, they developed a new approach to the way that crews would communicate with each other during a flight which ensured that all communication was clear, unambiguous, appropriate, and fully understood by all parties involved. It was called Crew Resource Management or CRM for short.

It over came situations where an experienced captain made a wrong decision, but junior crew felt unable to challenge it.

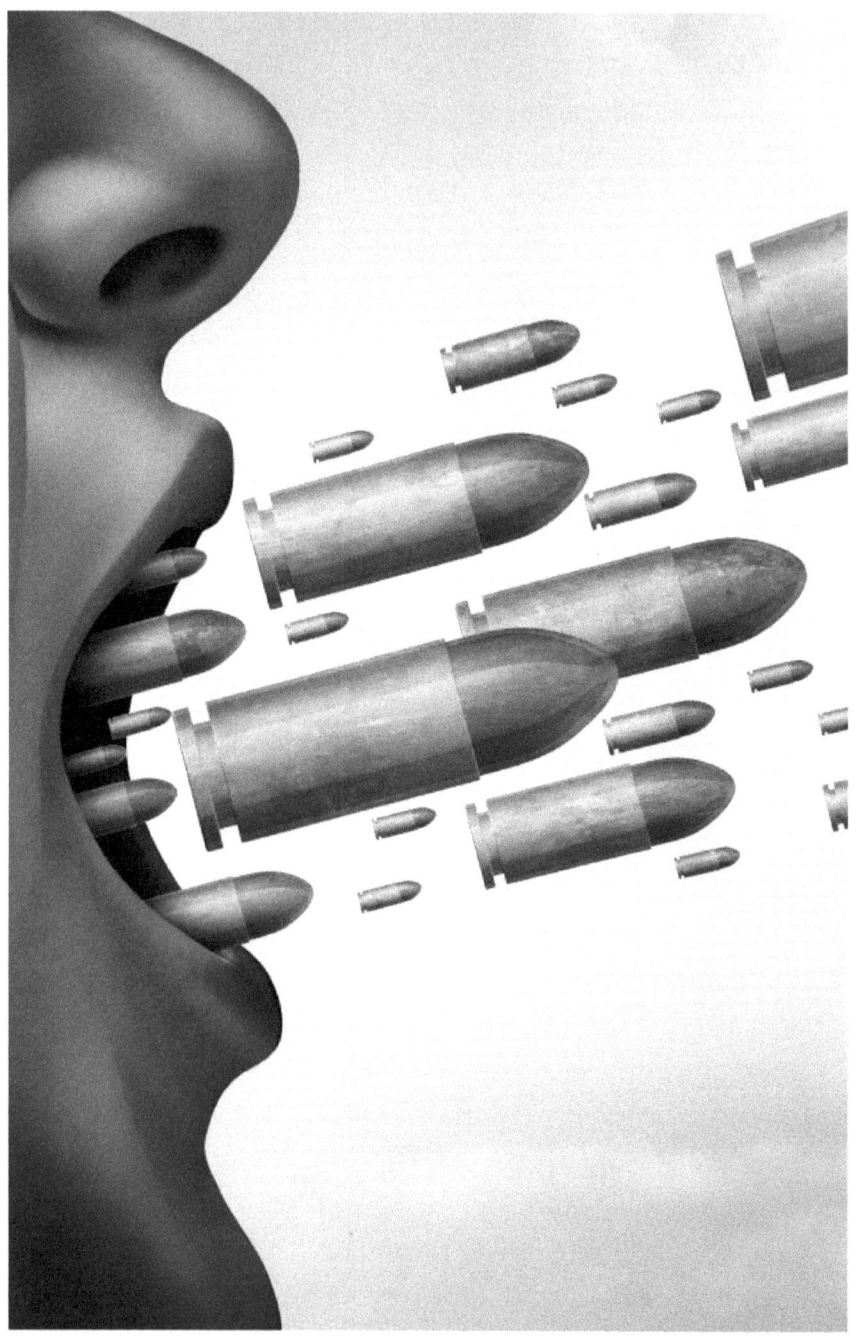

It overcame situations where people assumed something was being done when it wasn't. It was a structured form of communication that was used by everyone which ensured that everyone was equally responsible for the right outcome. And it worked. The number of unnecessary accidents fell dramatically and because everyone was using their words better.

What is your intent?

What is our Intent when using words? Are there underlying messages we are trying to communicate? Do we have another agenda hidden in what we are saying? Very often we don't take the time to think. We just respond. However, there are many situations in life and in business where we do not have the luxury of just saying what we think. There are situations where the precise use of communication is essential. Where it can mean life or death.

If we were being honest, we spend most of our time, when we are talking, "Shooting from the lip" - or speaking without really thinking about what we are saying. As a result, the outcomes of our conversations are not always what we would have wished. But this needn't be the case.

Instead of leaving things to chance, why not increase the possibility of a positive outcome, by paying more attention to the words you use? Some words will help, other words will not. So start with the end in mind.

THE BEST OF US MUST SOMETIMES EAT OUR WORDS.

J. K. Rowling

What outcome do you want from a conversation? What words will resonate with the person you are talking to, and what words will irritate them?

Always put yourself in the shoes of the other person. What do they need to hear in order to agree to what you are saying. How can you talk in terms of a win-win outcome? How can you create a desire in their mind for them to want to help you achieve what you want. It is all down to the words you choose to use.

> **INSULTS ARE THE ARGUMENTS EMPLOYED BY THOSE WHO ARE IN THE WRONG.**
>
> *Jean-Jacques Rousseau*

Chapter Twelve

WORDS AT HOME

I once heard somebody ask a question, "If you were to lock your wife and your dog in the boot of a car, and left them for an hour, when you came back which one would be pleased to see you?". The answer is dog, of course! You can be certain that your wife would be communicating in a robust and unambiguous matter which would leave you in no doubt of what she felt about the situation! The dog is just pleased to see you.

One of the most challenging places to have good and open conversations is at home with our families. Life gets complicated! Many people find it difficult to talk about family matters without being judgemental. Imagine you have just arrived home, a little later than planned, will you be greeted with the same enthusiasm as your dog, or might there be a hint of criticism or even anger over your late arrival? Is this familiar?

Most people would react instinctively and be defensive or even angry in return. What might have started as a minor challenge could easily escalate into a full blow row or even worse.

> **JUDGE A MAN BY HIS QUESTIONS RATHER THAN HIS ANSWERS.**
>
> *Voltaire*

The entire evening could so easily be ruined and everyone would go to bed unhappy. It can happen so easily.

Very often we are taken unawares, and can be challenged to respond without having any time to think of an appropriate response.

As a result, we just 'shoot from the lip' in defence. Not the best way of achieving a positive outcome!

In such circumstances you need a strategy to give you time to recover and think. Even a microsecond of decision making tends to dramatically improve the final outcome.

One strategy I find can be very effective is to repeat the question back to the person. This has two benefits. First, you are demonstrating that it is important to you that you clearly understand what they meant.

Secondly, you are giving them an opportunity to think about what they said, and possibly even re-frame the question in a different way. You are giving you both a moment to think about the way that the conversation could proceed and also what the outcome could be. Nobody likes to be challenged when they arrive late. There could be many perfectly legitimate reasons for it.

He that is good for making excuses is seldom good for anything else.

Benjamin Franklin

For example;

1. I was very busy at the office.
2. There was a traffic jam on the highway.
3. A very important customer was calling.
4. One of my colleges needed my input directly.
5. I forgot the time.
6. There was a bad driver in front of me, so he kept me on the road a little longer, so I could not be here on time.
7. If you would have any idea about my work, you would know. (assuming that you don't know)
8. Our company is in bad weather, so I did have to stay longer.
9. There was a very important meeting, and I needed to be there.
10. My stomach was feeling bad, so I spend a lot of time in the rest room.
11. My boss called me in his office.

Whatever the reason, it is how you respond next, that will determine what kind of evening your are going to have! Should you react defensively? Should you meet her head on in an aggressive way? Should you react calmly and concerned? After all, there may be circumstances that you don't yet know about which could more than justify the question.

> TRUST IS THE GLUE OF LIFE. IT'S THE MOST ESSENTIAL INGREDIENT IN EFFECTIVE COMMUNICATION. IT'S THE FOUNDATIONAL PRINCIPLE THAT HOLDS ALL RELATIONSHIPS.
>
> *Stephen Covey*

Never prejudge any situation, even though it might appear obvious. Always give people the opportunity to explain themselves rather than jump to conclusions.

Answer her question with one of your own to help you understand what is in her mind.

Demonstrate that you care about her and want to be supportive. With luck that will take the heat out of the situation.

When we do arrive home late, rather than engaging in a negative, defensive and hurtful conversation, we can use that dangerous moment, to demonstrate that we care and how much that person means to us. If we have gone out of our way in the past, to do this, then these potential communication flashpoints can be easily defused.

Good long-term relationships are built on good communication and the vocabulary we use in our conversations.

Over time, we get to know those words and phrases that hurt our partners the most and uses them when we want to make them feel uncomfortable. Do you know what words hurt and what words heal? The ones you choose will determine what happens next.

A WORD OF ENCOURAGEMENT FROM A TEACHER TO A CHILD CAN CHANGE A LIFE. A WORD OF ENCOURAGEMENT FROM A SPOUSE CAN SAVE A MARRIAGE. A WORD OF ENCOURAGEMENT FROM A LEADER CAN INSPIRE A PERSON TO REACH HER POTENTIAL.

John C. Maxwell

Chapter Thirteen

TALKING TO CHILDREN AND TEENAGERS

How much time do you spend with your kids at home? The answer is never enough! Children crave the love of a parent. It means more to them than anything else and is an essential part of helping them to grow into balanced adults.

However, it is an unfortunate fact of life that the one time that children want our attention the most, is the moment we arrive home from an long and stressful day at work. They have probably spent all day looking forward to seeing you and telling you about all the things they have done at school.

You cannot believe the deep disappointment they feel when you don't find time for them and turn them away.

There is a real art in being both a parent and also a best friend. Someone they can confide in and share with. Someone they can trust and who is their role model. Bringing up children is such a huge responsibility.

PARENTS ARE THE ULTIMATE ROLE MODELS FOR CHILDREN. EVERY WORD, MOVEMENT AND ACTION HAS AN EFFECT. NO OTHER PERSON OR OUTSIDE FORCE HAS A GREATER INFLUENCE ON A CHILD THAN THE PARENT.

Bob Keeshan

Parents often complain about how difficult teenagers are to talk to, but the seeds of that started much earlier when you were not there for them when they needed you.

How many times have your children asked you to play with them, but you made a polite excuse about still having some work to do. Looking back, just how important was that report or email compared with a little precious time with your kids? We can get our priorities all wrong. It is back to the two briefcases again!

It we are to enjoy a happy and supportive family life, then good communication is at the heart of it.

Giving the right attention at the right moment starts by deciding on your priority and what is most important thing at any one moment. Some things won't keep, some things can. You choose!

Your children want a bedtime story or even just a little bit of one-to-one time to show them that you care. So often you push them to one side, and in doing to, sow the seeds of future relationship problems.

Good communication with our loved ones is about living in the now, in the present.

There are only two lasting bequests we can hope to give our children. One of these is roots, the other, wings.

Johann Wolfgang von Goethe

Choosing to give them quality time. Demonstrating that we care about them. When you really care, you never have to worry about using the right words. they come naturally.

Out time is our most precious possession. It is a finite resource and it is ticking away all of the time. We certainly do not have enough of it to waste. Use it wisely with the people who really matter to you.

One of the reasons why so many of us find it difficult to enjoy an open and positive level of communication with our children and teenagers is that we put up barriers to them by being judgemental. If children learn by experience that a parent is going to react in a certain way, they will see no point in having that conversation. If we make ourselves difficult to communicate with, and reinforce that by not being open minded and not prepared to listen. We should not be surprised that they don't see that value in talking to us. We have trained them not to!

The most important rule is to listen more than we speak. That is why we have two ears and one mouth! If we make a deliberate choice to allow someone to speak without interrupting them, or being judgemental, then we become the sort of person they want to speak to. It is up to us, not them.

> **A DIVORCE IS LIKE AN AMPUTATION: YOU SURVIVE IT, BUT THERE'S LESS OF YOU.**
>
> *Margaret Atwood*

By the way, always hire a teenager whilst they still know everything. It won't last!

Vocabulary give us more options to convey the strength of our feelings. Limited vocabulary give us limited choices. With some people they only have the binary choice of being happy or furious - with nothing in between.

With your partner, what level of hostilities are you having? For example, instead of having a row or a fight, you could have a simple disagreement, a misunderstanding, a tiff, a quarrel, or a debate. What is the outcome you would prefer, a 'kiss and make up' or a divorce?

> **A CHILD WHO IS ALLOWED TO BE DISRESPECTFUL TO HIS PARENTS WILL NOT HAVE TRUE RESPECT FOR ANYONE.**
>
> *Billy Graham*

Parenting

It is sad to see when the loving bond between parents and children is under threat. When parents go from being the child's best friend, teacher, mentor and playmate to becoming the enemy. This is invariably down to a breakdown in communication.

From a parents perspective, bringing up a child is an almost impossible task. How can you stay friends when you also have to make and enforce the rules of the house, monitor screen time, protect them from danger and set curfews?

Is it even possible to maintain a positive relationship? Of course it doesn't help that they speak another language. There is no definitive dictionary definition of 'Teen Speak' probably because it is evolving all the time. The only objective is to make teen-to-teen communication completely incomprehensible to adults. In their world hot is cool and wicked is good. What chance do you stand?

Of course, this is not a new phenomenon. Cockney rhyming slang was developed to enable locals to communicate without outsiders knowing what was being said. Who could even guess that going to buy a 'Whistle' actually meant, going to buy a suit. (Whistle and Flute = suit). Up the 'apples' meant on the floor above (apples and pairs = stairs). This masked use of language has been going on for years.

Many professions, like the legal profession, have developed so many unique phrases, mostly in Latin, that only an insider knows what is being said. 'Teen Speak' is no different!

If teenagers feel they are being judged and the subject of criticism, they simply won't engage in conversations. Years of trust can be lost overnight when a parent chooses to confront rather than listen and converse. The earlier you can build a deep connection based on good listening and good support, the easier it will be to maintain this in later years. It is sometimes helpful to remember that you are a retired teenager. How easy were you to talk to? Hmmm?

On the other side of the coin, many married couples think nothing of having word fights in front of their children. Of themselves, they may mean nothing at the time, but never underestimate the deep unease that these bitter rows can have on children. I have seen many children have deep mental scars from having witnessed such angry scenes.

Children are learning behaviours from us all of the time that could well surface and re-emerge in later life. Never underestimate the effects of what you are teaching them.

Of course, all parents want the best for their children, don't we? They now have the benefit of experience.

They know where they went wrong and are determined that their children should not fall into the same traps. But how to do that without them getting upset and pushing them away.

The best way to start any conversation is with a question. It is the fastest way to find out what the other person is thinking and feeling. Questions can be inviting, intriguing, challenging, shocking, amusing, quirky or even threatening. We need to decide the reaction we want.

> **NO ONE IS DUMB WHO IS CURIOUS. THE PEOPLE WHO DON'T ASK QUESTIONS REMAIN CLUELESS THROUGHOUT THEIR LIVES.**
>
> *Neil deGrasse Tyson*

> **THE KEY IS TO KEEP COMPANY ONLY WITH PEOPLE WHO UPLIFT YOU, WHOSE PRESENCE CALLS FORTH YOUR BEST.**
>
> *Epictetus*

Chapter Fourteen

CORPORATE CULTURE

We have all heard the saying, "You can judge people by the company they keep." I would go one further. I believe you can judge a company by the people they keep. Long service is a sign that an organisation has got things right.

Where people feel appreciated, are recognised for their contribution, and have a purpose, why would they leave? Having worked in many top European and international companies, I believe that you can tell how successful they will be by the language that emanates from the top.

Some managers are Excel terrorists. They communicate with spreadsheets and commands. Their focus is on numbers, graphs and shareholders, not on the people that are responsible for delivering them. not surprisingly, staff do not feel that they matter and there is little loyalty to the organisation.

It is the Language of Leadership and the corporate vocabulary that determine the success and indeed, the longevity of the business.

Whilst many organisations are so focussed on the bottom line that they forget the importance of their people, there are many organisations who do get it spectacularly right.

> **THE ART OF COMMUNICATION IS THE LANGUAGE OF LEADERSHIP.**
>
> *James Humes*

I know of a sales organisation with offices scattered our the UK and Ireland that was constantly recruiting and training sales people. The chances of the managing director ever meeting them was slim, however the corporate culture of the organisation was such that each person felt valued and noticed right from the beginning.

After graduation for the training course, the new sales people were let loose on the world and went out to do in home sales presentation. Despite their lack of experience, many of them would trip over a sale - usually despite themselves rather than because of it. Some people were going to buy anyway no matter who did the presentation.

Three days later, and completely unexpectedly, the salesman would receive in the post a hand written note of congratulations and a bottle of Champagne from the managing director. How do you think that made them feel about their job and also the company? To be recognised by the person at the top of the company, who had never met them, but knew what they were doing, was a great boost. Those handwritten notes of congratulation were always kept and treasured. A great example of an empowering corporate culture, that encouraged loyalty and inspired people to do their best. A few well chosen words can do amazing things.

I have seen in many successful organisations the philosophy of looking out for people doing something right, and then recognising them for doing so.

FEELING GRATITUDE AND NOT EXPRESSING IT IS LIKE WRAPPING A PRESENT AND NOT GIVING IT.

William Arthur Ward

The culture of making people feel great about what they are doing, cost nothing. It is just using the right words and the right time, to the right people.

However, I have seen other organisations try and do this in a formulaic and predictable way that has the opposite results and make the company less credible rather than more.

Just how motivational is being "Employee of the Month" and having your name on a plaque, if you feel that you have done nothing to deserve it? It is probably worse than getting second prize in a beauty contest!

Some organisations spend stupid amounts of money on employee recognition programmes, and yet fail to do the basics of good day to day communication, treating people like human beings. You need to have all the basics in place first, or you are just throwing money away. In my view for recognition to work at a deep level it has to tick the following boxes. My "G.U.I.D.E." to effective recognition.

Use this G.U.I.D.E. to measure the way you are planning to recognise an individual or a team to test whether it is going to achieve the results you are hoping for. It you cannot tick each of these boxes, then you should think again!

Don't work for recognition, but do work worthy of recognition.

H. Jackson Brown, Jr.

The G.U.I.D.E. to Recognition

G   First, any recognition has to be Genuine. If it is not this will be completely obvious to the recipient who will not take it seriously, and probably be annoyed.

U   U is for Unexpected. Surprise is the key to effective recognition. If you know its coming, and if it is predicable, it will never have the same impact.

I   I It has to be In Writing. The spoken word is all well and good, but you can't show this to your partner nor can you put in on the mantelpiece for the children to see. All recognition has to have physical proof.

D   D "D" id for Deserved. If the recipient knows that there is another agenda for giving them recognition it causes distrust and confusion. Recognition only where it is truly deserved.

E   E is for Empowering. Will this recognition make them feel good? Will it spur them one to greater things? Or is the manager trying to get at someone else by recognising you instead. People are very sensitive to motive.

LEADERSHIP IS NOT A POPULARITY CONTEST; IT'S ABOUT LEAVING YOUR EGO AT THE DOOR. THE NAME OF THE GAME IS TO LEAD WITHOUT A TITLE.

Robin S. Sharma

Any recognition can have the opposite results it it is not genuine and not properly thought through.

In every company, everything starts at the top. All communications filter down. The words of the Chief Executive are read extremely carefully by everyone in order to find clues as to what is happening - and how it affects them. They are studying not just the words, but also what is in between the lines that wasn't said.

The words used by the CEO are a mirror on their thoughts, their values, their vision and their focus. These words are then taken up by the directors and heads of divisions. They filter down to the departmental heads and the line managers.

Everybody is singing from the same hymn sheet and is reflecting the culture of the company - as led from the top.

The key point here is that, if you want to change the fundamental nature of a company, there is no point at all in doing a training programme with the staff at the bottom of the pyramid. It is a complete waste of time. You need to start at the top.

If you can change the thinking and the vocabulary of the CEO, you can change the entire organisation. The right words can achieve truly amazing results.

> **A POSITIVE ATTITUDE CAUSES A CHAIN REACTION OF POSITIVE THOUGHTS, EVENTS AND OUTCOMES. IT IS A CATALYST AND IT SPARKS EXTRAORDINARY RESULTS.**
>
> *Wade Boggs*

The Ego has landed

All of us have an ego. It is another word for our conscious mind, the part of your identity that you consider your "self." If you say someone has "a big ego," then you are saying he is too full of himself.

It is very often the case that people with a big ego are better at convincing others of their worth and are more likely to end of at the top of an organisation. Whether they are the right person to lead that company is a different matter.

Your ego is not your amigo!

With an ego can come the conviction that they are right at all time and incapable of making mistakes. Their role as a leader is to tell people what to do, rather than listen to what they have to say. The other side of the coin is that, when people know that you are not listening, they don't tell you what you need to know, but rather what you want to hear. Not a recipe for long term success.

IMPRISONED BY WORDS

I have worked within some companies that are literally grinding to a halt. An inertia has crept in where people keep

their heads down and just do their jobs without rocking the boat.

The emphasis is on keeping the job and staying in their comfort zone. With no momentum and engagement coming from managers, (who also have the same mindset) the business just trundles on, going nowhere. And in today's competitive marketplace, there is always a competitor just around the corner who has their eyes on your customers.

When working in an organisation, I will always start at the top. I remember visiting a CEO of a large company. I knocked on his door and heard him say "Enter!". So I did. He was standing in the centre of the room with his back to me, looking out of a big window. I came in and waited, but he didn't turn round.

I though to myself, "I'll wait for him to turn round" but he didn't. He then said, "You can start."

"Yes," I said, "I know I can start. I can talk with you or without you, but I am not going to talk to the back of you. I want to see your face. If I am not going to see your face, then I'm out of here. your call." He turned round. "Ah, I like this" he said "Have a seat, Have a coffee." He was just testing me.

We then had a good conversation. Fundamentally, he was a good guy, but his first level of mangers were not. Whether it was his communication style or his ego, they just told him what they thought he wanted to hear, not what was actually happening. any leader is only as good as the information he has on which to base decisions.

You can only be an effective leader if you create a culture in which open communication is both possible and encouraged. Anything less is a recipe for disaster.

Conversations with colleagues

All of us need to find ourselves in a supportive and positive environment surrounded with people who share our vision and values. There are many work situations where none of the above are present and you feel that you just don't fit in. This can be a lonely space.

Many offices are negative places where people seem to delight in saying bad things about their company, their boss and their colleagues. How tempting is it to join that 'pity party' and share negatives. It can sometime be a competition to see who can share the most negative story. If you are new to an organisation, people will want to drag you down to their level, rather than letting you show them up for what they really are.

No matter what the temptation is to want to belong, once you start entertaining negatives, it is a downward slope from there which can only do you damage not good. But not for you, you are that person that can create a shift in their paradigm. Your choice of words and the attitude that goes with them is the only thing that you have any control over.

You have no control over what other people say or do. You have no control over your boss, you have no control over the company or its customers. Whatever happens, the only thing that you have control over is yourself and the attitude you bring to bear on any given situation. Fortunately this is enough. The attitude you bring to any situation is your choice. This will manifest itself in the words you use. Use them wisely!

If you consciously want to have a bad day, then start it by sharing negatives with other people. We always attract what we think about and what we talk about the most. It is the Law of Attraction. If you make the choice to think positively and to talk positively,, you will always attract good things into your life.

So whether you have a good day or not, is your choice.

> **Your customers are the lifeblood of your business. Their needs and wants impact every aspect of your business, from product development to content marketing to sales to customer service.**
>
> *John Rampton*

Communicating with Customers

I have heard it said, half in jest, half in earnest that, if it wasn't for the customers, this would be a great place to work. The truth is that customers can be very annoying!

Customers demand attention. They create problems. They want things done right away. Basically, they have no understanding of the importance of tea breaks or lunch breaks. They disrupt everything!

Is this really the case? Or is it due to misunderstanding on our part? Could it be that we are not fully aware about their real needs and expectations? Without customers we do not have a business or an income, so we need to put them first.

This easy to say, but not easy to do. It requires us to be observant, knowledgeable and proactive in identifying their needs. Everyone appreciates a sales person who anticipates what they want. Each customer presents us with an opportunity to create a positive moment for them in their day. It could be the only positive interaction they had!

SALES ARE CONTINGENT UPON THE ATTITUDE OF THE SALESMAN - NOT THE ATTITUDE OF THE PROSPECT.

W. Clement Stone

Each 'touch point' one is an opportunity to demonstrate your knowledge, your enthusiasm and your professionalism. A customer, well looked after, can be the start of a long, strong and profitable relationship. So what is the secret to communicating with customers?

Firstly, never assume anything. Always ask. To 'assume' is to make an 'ass' out of 'u' and 'me'.

Many customer relationships go wrong because they were not asked the right questions in the first place. Perfect your listening skills. Good selling is not about talking at someone, it is about getting a deep knowledge of their needs and the reason for those needs. Only then can you help them to find the right solution for them..

The one reason that puts potential customers off from doing business with an organisation, is that they felt that they were not appreciated or fully understood.

Don't forget that the sales process is not just a transaction, but it should be the start of a long term relationship. It starts with the sale but shouldn't end there. People always buy people first before they buy what they are selling.

It is a shame to say the noble art of salesmanship is vanishing and the skills surrounding it are no longer passed down within organisations. So much experience has been lost and has a fundamental appreciation of what the sales process consists of.

> **THE GREATEST DECEPTION MEN SUFFER IS FROM THEIR OWN OPINIONS.**
>
> *Leonardo da Vinci*

The same principles applies whether you are selling person to person or online.

Some of these great principles of salesmanship were created in 1936 by Dale Carnegie in his multimillion best-selling book "How to Win Friends and Influence People". The book remains in print and has never been bettered.

One of the main principles in sales is to be a good listener. Become genuinely interested in the other person. Indeed, let them do most of the talking. Let them tell you why they want what you are selling and what difference it will make to them. Far more powerful coming from them than coming from you. Discovering the real needs opens lots of doors.

Show respect for the other person's opinions. Never tell anyone that they are wrong. Always talk about benefits in terms of their individual needs and the value to them. Above all, be genuine and look at everything through their eyes and their interests.

What do you want to achieve for your customer? Will they will be your next best reference?

If you don't aim high enough you will never get there. So, what is getting in the way when you mention the word customer? What is the first thought you have when you read the word customer?

The simple act of paying attention can take you a long way.

Keanu Reeves

I am just curious about your first thought. Is it about money, happiness, satisfaction, reference, client, ambassador, freedom, experience, whatever word you think of, they are all good? It depends on how you want to achieve this for the customer.

Of course, no two people are the same, and it will be your listening skills that will help you to respond appropriately.

- What goes through your mind when you see a customer?
- Do you see them as a profit centre, or as a person?
- Do you just see a transaction or do you see someone who could be your best ambassador ever.

How well are you able to listen to your customer? Do you really hear what they are trying to tell you, or do you just hear what you want to hear? Do you give them enough time to express their needs or are you rushing them?

How engaged are you with with your work? Or are you just doing your job and waiting till its time to go home? What do you think that the customers see in you? Do they see your energy, enthusiasm and interest in them? Or do they spot your reluctance to engage with them?

Do you engage them in conversation? Do you ask feedback questions. For example, "Did you find what you are looking for? "Did it meet up to your expectations?"

Do you pay genuine compliments? "That looks really good on you!" "Do you thank them for shopping with you?"

The only true wisdom is in knowing you know nothing.

Socrates

Does your customer compliment you and the service you gave? What are they likely to say about you and your company to their friends?

Positive feedback gets you noticed.

We dare not assume what our customers think or what they want, we need them to tell us. For them to do so, we need to ask them the right questions.

I never forget the next story. I was invited at one of my friends' house for a birthday party and the owner asked me what I do in my daily profession. I told him about coaching, training and psychology in a broader spectrum. Then all of a sudden, he told me that he was such a great salesperson that he could not be taught any new skills because of his expertise throughout his life. I thought to myself, "How fascinating! In my belief this man thinks he is the finished product and not a work in progress - as we all are." I answered and nodded yes, I understand and if this is your thought then it is just okay. Then he kept on talking about it and he at least repeated this four times that he was the best salesperson in the whole area and that there would be nobody out there to teach him some new skills.

After the fourth time I asked him a question about his listening skills. I asked him if he had a specific reason telling me this four times in a row that he didn't need any training. He answered that he did not have any specific reason for it.

Why did you ask he said?

My answer was, because I gave you the same answer four times in a row and you kept on explaining the same thing.

He was the owner in cosmetics and all the ingredients for hair cutters. I kept listening and after 30 minutes I asked him a question about his employees, what sort of training did he give to his sales team to keep their skills at their best? He was very strong with his answer which you can probably guess! "They don't need it!" he answered, "I have trained them and that's all they need." Could it be that he wanted to maintain his status as the top sales person by depriving his salesman of training so as not to outshine him? You wonder!

Chapter Fifteen
PREPARING FOR A JOB INTERVIEW

JOB INTERVIEWS

With a job interview, the product you are selling is yourself. The question you need to know is, what are they in the market to buy? Are you the person they are looking for? You will need to listen very carefully to pick up clues.

The more you can research the company you are looking to join, the better. Research is never wasted. You could discover that this is the last company on earth that you would want to be a part of, or just the opposite! Better know that now, than a year down the line. Be all over their websites like a rash! Write down questions of your own about the company. Who are their competition? And make sure to ask them questions during a job interview. This will give you the opportunity to discover if it's a two way street and whether you might love to work in that company.

Job interviews are a two way street. You are selling, they are buying. The only challenge is that you may not know precisely what criteria they are going to measure you against. So do not be afraid to ask questions.

PERFECTION IS NOT ATTAINABLE, BUT IF WE CHASE PERFECTION WE CAN CATCH EXCELLENCE.

Vince Lombardi

Never try to be somebody you are not. It will always backfire.

When creating your CV, look at it as a 'portfolio career' in which everything you have done in the past could be seen as a preparation for this new job. List not just the jobs you have done, but the skills and experiences you got from each one. Your potential employer will want to see the skill-sets you have acquired on your journey. There may even be a better job that you are perfectly qualified for. There are no prizes for hiding your light under a bushel!

If you have ever conducted interviews yourself you will know what a difficult job it can be. Very often there will be very little to choose between a number of candidates. So think about how you can stand out and be remembered. You will need to chose your words and deliver them with confidence. Avoid anything that is negative. Remember that they are looking for someone for the long-term not the short-term. Do not give them any cause to doubt your commitment to the company.

Most important of all, you cannot be over prepared. That preparation includes your mindset. Let your positive attitude shine through!

Never forget, you only have one chance to make a first impression!

NO ONE HAS A GREATER ASSET FOR HIS BUSINESS THAN A MAN'S PRIDE IN HIS WORK.

Hosea Ballou

Communicating with Managers

One of the biggest challenges in any growing business is that there comes a time when the number of staff have grown to a point where none of the mangers know them all. There are just too many of them or they are no longer in the one place.. At that point, communication inevitably becomes less personal and driven by memos or emails.

It has been said that people are promoted to their level of incompetence. It is known as the Peter Principle. It is based on the flawed premise that if somebody is a good engineer or a good technical specialist, they will automatically be a good manager. So they get promoted from a place that they were perfectly qualified, to a role in which they have no qualifications at all. Hence, to the level of incompetence.

The interesting thing is that companies are filled with managers who have no idea what the role means. So often, in that situation, an individual thinks back to their experience of working for a manager in the past - good or bad, and tried to emulate their behaviour. Often with disastrous results.

> The key to being a good manager is keeping the people who hate me away from those who are still undecided.

Casey Stengel

Another thing that gets in the way is ego and an inflated sense of self-worth. Not the best quality to build an effective team with!

So, the first thing to do to communicate with your manager is to know your manager.

- What sort of manager are they?
- What are their management styles?
- What do they need of you?
- What role do they need you to perform in the team?
- What will make their life easier?
- How can you build rapport?
- What are their pet hates?

Communication in a business environment is very different to a social or family environment. It needs to be;

- Precise
- Follow a prescribed style
- Factual
- Free of emotion
- Devoid of personal opinion, likes and dislikes
- Fit for purpose

Your vocabulary will include the words and phrases that you will have picked up from others in the business.

Be a sponge to soak up the words which your manager wants to hear that will help him to know you and understand what he is looking for.

> A MAN'S CHARACTER MAY BE LEARNED FROM THE ADJECTIVES WHICH HE HABITUALLY USES IN CONVERSATION.
>
> *Mark Twain*

Chapter Sixteen
COMMUNICATING AS A MANAGER

One of the most difficult transitions to make in a career is when someone is promoted from being a normal employee to becoming a manager. It is a real quantum leap in terms of the way they now communicate, and the way people now communicate with them.

It is really difficult to move from being just 'one of the boys' to becoming the person in charge. It can be painful when the people you have been friends with now see you in a completely different way and now exclude you from the friendly chats that you used to have around the water cooler. Some of them may feel jealous at your promotion and think that they should have got the job. Others will try and test you and not take your new role seriously. It can often be difficult to exert your new authority and to give instructions to people who still see you as the employee you used to be. If ever there was a time for good communication, this is it!

The only way you can get anyone to do anything is if they want to do it. If you can create that 'want' you will succeed far better that if you simply bark orders at people.

A MANAGER IS NOT A PERSON WHO CAN DO THE WORK BETTER THAN HIS MEN; HE IS A PERSON WHO CAN GET HIS MEN TO DO THE WORK BETTER THAN HE CAN.

Frederick W. Smith

Many people, when promoted to a managerial role, feel that they have to behave differently but have no idea what that means. Often they will think back to a manager they worked for in the past and use the way that they behaved, as a role model. If that manager had poor qualities, this could be a disaster!

All of a sudden you cease to be your authentic self and take on a new personality, a new attitude and a new vocabulary. No wonder you are not taken seriously.

In any office, it is the manager that sets the tone and creates the atmosphere. This can be positive or negative, supportive or confrontational. As a manager, people will look to you for what is acceptable and what isn't. They will look at your communication style and adopt it for themselves. In the same way that you will be influenced by the values and attitudes of your senior managers and directors, so they will be influenced by yours. What a wonderful opportunity you have to create a warm, supportive and empowering workplace! Never before have your choice of words been more important!

If the office has been a negative place before, full of gossip and back biting, overtime you can transform it by your example.

Your words could indeed change the lives of your colleagues if you make the decision to be both a manager and also an inspirational leader.

> **Always be your true self, and surround yourself with positive and supportive people.**
>
> *Amanda Lepore*

To succeed as a manager you need to choose what sort of manager you want to be. Will you be a dictator? Will you let your ego take over and believe you are better than everyone else? Will you take responsibility for creating a supportive space that people enjoy working in? The choice is yours.

Are you a Manager, or a Man-ager?

Being given the title of Manager doesn't automatically give someone all of the necessary skills, attitudes, strategies and human relations to be a success in their role. Rarely is there any training given in what a good manager should do or how they should behave. As a result, few people find success in being a manager right from the start.

I often joke about the difference between a manager and a man-ager. Nobody comes to work to be 'aged' but that is often the case when a working environment feels uncaring, stressful, toxic, or negative. In reality, the art of being a good manager is very much linked to your communication style and your choice of words.

What we see nowadays are many different people who call themselves a manager but with no real idea of what they need to do to be successful in that role.

> **THERE ARE TIMES WHEN EVEN THE BEST MANAGER IS LIKE THE LITTLE BOY WITH THE BIG DOG, WAITING TO SEE WHERE THE DOG WANTS TO GO SO HE CAN TAKE HIM THERE.**
>
> *Lee Iacocca*

Of course, there is always pressure on managers to achieve targets, get their teams to work efficiently and in harmony and to achieve the objectives they have been given.

What I discovered is that there are two different type of managers, Managers and man-AGERS.

What are the qualities of a Manager?

1. A real manager takes care about people and works together with them as a team.
2. Makes a person feel comfortable and important.
3. Makes it possible that a person can grow.
4. Is not afraid of hiring people who are much better than he or she is.
5. He or she does have a total overview, not only for themselves but also for others.
6. They are not afraid of the success of what their employees achieve.
7. Is capable of trusting people and guiding them through the company.
8. Sees failures as an option to grow.
9. Is not afraid to stand up for his or her opinion.

When I'm hiring someone I look for magic and a spark. Little things that intuitively give me a gut feeling that this person will go to the ends of the earth to accomplish the task at hand.

Tommy Mottola

Chapter Seventeen
CHOOSING YOUR WORDS

We are all far better communicators than we believe we are. It is usually only when our communications go wrong, or there is a misunderstanding or a row, that we get frustrated with ourselves. Very often this comes from our belief that we are just delivering a message, rather than we are entering into a dialogue. One way communication, rather than two way communication.

It is always the responsibility of the person communicating to ensure that their message is received and understood, rather the responsibility of the person on the receiving end. We know what we said, but what we don't know is what the other person heard. It may be completely different!

In a restaurant, a waiter taking an order will always repeat it back to the diner just to check if he had heard the order correctly.

During any conversation, we need to reassure ourselves of the same thing. We need to listen and to give the other person the opportunity of agreeing or disagreeing with us.

I once took part in an induction programme run by a large company. This programme was very important to the employees as it covered essential information about company policy, procedures, practices, health and safety.

> LET US MAKE A SPECIAL EFFORT TO STOP COMMUNICATING WITH EACH OTHER, SO WE CAN HAVE SOME CONVERSATION.
>
> *Mark Twain*

This was an organisation that had a lot of equipment, forklift trucks, and material handling. It was vital that every employee understood their role and the inherent dangers in their working environment.

However, the management saw the induction programme as a chore. It took management time to deliver it which was an interruption to their day. They were only doing it because they had to.

The sheer volume of information that needed to be delivered was vast. Far more than could be effectively delivered in the time available. As a result, the delivery was rushed and many thing glossed over. It was delivered as a monotone talk with no audio visual aids. Frankly it was boring! At the end of the session, all the participants were completely overwhelmed with information that little of it sunk in and even less was remembered. However, in the eyes of the management, they had done their duty and could tick that box. It was the worst kind of one way communication.

I was able to help them transform their induction process and make it far more effective by simply using all of the practical communication principles in this book.

In transferring information to people you need to:
- Tell people what you are going to tell them
- Then tell it to them
- Follow that by telling them what you told them
- And then ask them what they heard

> **THE CULTURE OF A WORKPLACE - AN ORGANISATION'S VALUES, NORMS AND PRACTICES - HAS A HUGE IMPACT ON OUR HAPPINESS AND SUCCESS.**
>
> *Adam Grant*

Each of those four steps are essential if you want to get your message across in such a way as it is remembered and acted upon.

But is is not just using good communication techniques, it is about the words themselves and where they come from.

Our choice of words betrays what we are thinking and the attitude we have chosen to adopt at that moment. To anyone listening to us, we are an open book.

If you embark on a conversation with a negative attitude, if you are angry or if you are aggressive, you should not expect the same outcome to that conversation as if you had started with an open mind, a positive attitude or in a caring manner. It is obvious! However, few of us stop to think, and just 'shoot from the lip'. Again.

The words we need to positively influence any situation will flow automatically, if our attitude is right and if we are focussed on helping the other person clearly understand our message - and giving them the opportunity to confirm that they have.

In reality, we all communicate better when we are in a positive mind-set. However, what most people don't realise is that this is a choice - and is nothing to do with the circumstances themselves.

> Data is not information, information is not knowledge, knowledge is not understanding, understanding is not wisdom.

Clifford Stoll

For example, in the UK, most conversations start with a reference to the weather. Why? I don't know. The weather is obvious to everyone. We all know what it is. Why people need to start each conversation with the obvious is a mystery to me. However, it is their choice of words that is interesting.

It was raining the other day as I went to meet a client. "It's a terrible day," he said to me as I entered his office. "Not at all," I replied, "It is a lovely day. it just happens to be raining!" He stopped and thought for a moment. "You're right." he said.

Why do we instinctively look for negatives to share, and invite people to share negatives back to us? To me it is a mystery. With so many positive and empowering things that could be said to start a conversation, why miss that opportunity and default to the gloomiest thing you can think of?

Or maybe we just didn't think and spoke automatically. Again!

Every interaction we have with someone is an opportunity to strengthen that relationship or to weaken it. Every time we talk to that person, whether on the phone, or in person is precious. Don't waste it on trivia. Use it to good effect.

> **What you see is not what others see. We inhabit parallel worlds of perception, bounded by our interests and experience. What is obvious to some is invisible to others.**
>
> *George Monbiot*

As Lao Tzuonce said

KINDNESS IN WORDS CREATES CONFIDENCE. KINDNESS IN THINKING CREATES PROFOUNDNESS. KINDNESS IN GIVING CREATES LOVE.

Speak well!

Jos

APPENDIX
JOS'S LIST OF POSITIVE WORDS

Positive Words Starting With the Letter A

1. **Absolutely** – with no qualification, restriction, or limitation
2. **Abundant** – existing or available in large quantities
3. **Accessible** – friendly and amicable to talk with
4. **Acclaimed** – publicly praised; celebrated
5. **Accommodative** – friendly and flexible
6. **Achievement** – an accomplishment
7. **Adaptive** – changing oneself according to the environment and the surroundings
8. **Admire** – look up to and feel impressed
9. **Adore** – to love someone very much
10. **Adulation** – very great admiration
11. **Affability** – having the tendency to be friendly
12. **Agathist** – a person who believes that all things tend towards the ultimate good
13. **Alive** – living
14. **Amuse** – impress
15. **Animated** – having liveliness shine through
16. **Approve** – officially agree to or accept as satisfactory
17. **Assure** – tell someone something to dispel any doubts

18. **Attractive** – being fascinating and mesmerizing
19. **Awesome** – something breathtakingly amazing

Positive Words Starting With the Letter B

20. **Baronial** – impressive in appearance
21. **Beaming** – radiating
22. **Beautiful** – having qualities that delight and please the senses
23. **Beguiling** – highly charming
24. **Beloved** – greatly loved
25. **Benign** – kind
26. **Best** – surpassing all others in quality or excellence
27. **Bewitching** – enchanting
28. **Boss** – slang for excellent
29. **Brainy** – smart
30. **Breathtaking** – awe-inspiring
31. **Bubbly** – full of cheerful high spirits

Positive Words Starting With the Letter C

32. **Centred** – goal-oriented
33. **Champion** – holding first place in a contest
34. **Charismatic** – possessing an extraordinary ability to attract
35. **Charming** – fascinating
36. **Cheerful** – having life or vigor or spirit

37. **Chic** – fashionable
38. **Chipper** – lively
39. **Chummy** – friendly
40. **Classy** – elegant
41. **Clever** – possessing quickness of intellect
42. **Colourful** – interesting
43. **Comical** – funny
44. **Communicative** – able to communicate in a good and productive way
45. **Constant** – steadfast in purpose
46. **Courageous** – possessing courage

Positive Words Starting With the Letter D

47. **Definite** – free from doubt
48. **Delectable** – greatly pleasing
49. **Delicious** –highly pleasing to the senses
50. **Delightful** – bringing pleasure

51. **Dependable** – worthy of trust or reliance
52. **Dignified** – respectable
53. **Divine** – heavenly
54. **Down-to-earth** – realistic
55. **Dreamy** – fantasy-like
56. **Dynamite** –outstanding

Positive Words Starting With the Letter E

57. **Ecstatic** – pleasurable
58. **Electrifying** – causing a surge of excitement or emotion
59. **Employable** – one who is qualified and ready to work
60. **Empowered** – having power or confidence to make relevant choices to one's situation
61. **Endearing** – making beloved
62. **Enjoyable** – pleasure or enjoyment
63. **Enriching** – something that improves or adds value
64. **Enthusiastic** – having or showing intense and eager enjoyment
65. **Enticing** – alluring
66. **Especial** – exceptional
67. **Excellent** – of the finest or highest quality
68. **Exciting** – stimulating interest
69. **Exhilarating** – making lively
70. **Exultant** – characterised by rejoicing

Positive Words Starting With the Letter F

71. **Fab** – extremely pleasing
72. **Fain** – pleased or willing under the circumstances
73. **Fantastic** – extraordinarily good or attractive
74. **Fashionable** – having refined taste in manners or dress.
75. **Favorite** – preferred before all others of the same kind

76. **Fearless** – bold and lacking fear
77. **Fetching** – capturing the interest
78. **Fiery** – passionate and burning strongly and brightly
79. **Friend** – a person whom one knows and with whom one has a bond of mutual affection
80. **Fun** – enjoyable

Positive Words Starting With the Letter G

81. **Gallant** – honourable and heroic
82. **Gay** — lighthearted and carefree
83. **Genuine** – authentic
84. **Gifted** – skillful or talented in some field
85. **Gleaming** – bright with a steady but dimmed shining or light
86. **Glittering** – impressively elaborate
87. **Gnarly** –outstanding
88. **Goodhearted** – generous
89. **Grandiose** – characterised by the greatness of intent
90. **Greatest** – highest in quality or size
91. **Gumptious** – having good judgment and perception

Positive Words Starting With the Letter H

92. **Happy** – marked by good luck
93. **Heavenly** – extremely pleasurable or good

94. **Honorable** – worthy of respect or honour
95. **Hospitable** – generous or favourable towards quests
96. **Humanitarian** – having concern for helping and improving welfare and happiness of humans
97. **Hypnotic** – attracting interest as if by spell

Positive Words Starting With the Letter I

98. **Ideal** – considered the best of its kind or highly satisfactory
99. **Imaginative** – creative
100. **Impeccable** – flawless
101. **Impressive** – anything that is or creates a remarkable or striking impression
102. **Incredible** – extraordinary good
103. **Innovative** – the creation of new things or ideas
104. **Insightful** – having or showing insight
105. **Inspiring** – encouraging
106. **Instinctive** – driven or acted by impulse and without thinking
107. **Intellectual** – clever
108. **Irresistible** – impossible to resist

Positive Words Starting With the Letter J

108. **Jammy** – lucky
109. **Jesting** – light-hearted

110. **Jolly** – full of good humor and merry spirits
111. **Jovial** – characterized by good cheer and hearty conviviality
112. **Joysome** – inspiring or causing gladness or joy
113. **Judicious** – exhibiting or having sound judgment
114. **Juicy** – enticing
115. **Just** – righteous

Positive Words Starting With the Letter K

116. **Keen** – intellectual quickness
117. **Kind-hearted** – having a friendly and cheerful disposition
118. **Knightly** – chivalrous
119. **Knockout** – strikingly impressive or attractive
120. **Knowledgeable** – intelligent

Positive Words Starting With the Letter L

121. **Laid-back** – easy-going
122. **Lambent** – softly brilliant
123. **Laudable** – praiseworthy
124. **Legendary** – extremely popular
125. **Level-headed** – rational

126. **Likable** – easy to like
127. **Lionhearted** – courageous
128. **Lively** – full of life
129. **Lovely** – full of love
130. **Luminous** – emitting light or full of light

Positive Words Starting With the Letter M

131. **Magical** – enchanting
132. **Magnetic** – having an ability or power to attract
133. **Magnificent** – splendid or elegant in appearance
134. **Majestic** – noble
135. **Marvellous** – extraordinarily great or good.
136. **Masterful** – very skilful or powerful
137. **Mindful** – attentive
138. **Miraculous** – so wonderful and astounding as to suggest a miracle
139. **Motivated** – enthusiastic striving toward a goal or action
140. **Moving** – capable of arousing deep emotion

Positive Words Starting With the Letter N

141. **Neighbourly** – exhibiting or having the qualities of a friendly neighbor
142. **Nifty** – very good

143. **Noble** – showing or having qualities of high moral, rank or dignity
144. **Numinous** – awe-inspiring

Positive Words Starting With the Letter O

145. **Obedient** – dutifully complying with the commands or instructions of those in authority
146. **Obliging** – showing readiness to do favours for others
147. **Observant** – paying close attention to details
148. **On-target** – accurate
149. **Open-hearted** – kind and generous
150. **Open-minded** – ready or receptive to new and different ideas
151. **Optimistic** – disposed to take the most favourable or hopeful view of the matter
152. **Orderly** – systematic
153. **Organized** – efficient or methodical in function or arrangement
154. **Original** – authentic
155. **Outgoing** – responsive and sociable to others
156. **Out-of-this-world** – extremely impressive or enjoyable
157. **Outstanding** – prominent or noticeable of others of its kind
158. **Overjoyed** – extremely happy and joyful

Positive Words Starting With the Letter P

159. **Pally** – friendly
160. **Paramount** – supreme
161. **Passionate** – having or showing powerful emotions
162. **Patient** – calm during difficult situations
163. **Peaceful** – not disturbed by turmoil
164. **Peachy** – splendid
165. **Peppy** – cheerful and vigorous
166. **Perceptive** – having or showing ability and keenness of perception
167. **Persevering** – constant in the execution of a purpose
168. **Persistent** – refusing to give up
169. **Personable** – pleasing in appearance or personality
170. **Persuasive** – convincing
171. **Phenomenal** – outstanding
172. **Philanthropic** – generous in assistance
173. **Picturesque** – quaintly attractive and charming; pretty as a picture
174. **Piquant** – charming or interesting
175. **Playful** – full of high spirits and fun
176. **Polished** – elegant
177. **Posh** – fashionable and smart
178. **Prized** – cherished
179. **Proactive** – acting in advance to deal with an expected difficulty or change
180. **Promising** – showing or having the possibility of achievement or excellence
181. **Proud** – feeling of self-respect or self-worth
182. **Punctual** – prompt

Positive Words Starting With The Letter Q

183. Queenly – a regal and distinguished woman
184. Quick-witted – mentally sharp, nimble and alert
185. Quirky – merry and unconventional

Positive Words Starting With The Letter R

186. **Rad** – excellent
187. **Radiant** – emanating great love, joy or happiness
188. **Rapturous** – filled with great joy or delight
189. **Razor-sharp** – extremely sharp; quick-witted or very clever
190. **Reassuring** – relieving anxiety and restoring confidence
191. **Recherche** – exquisite
192. **Recommendable** – worthy of praise or to be recommended
193. **Refulgent** – radiant
194. **Reliable** – trustworthy
195. **Remarkable** – worthy of notice or consideration
196. **Resilient** – characterized by the ability to recover readily from misfortune
197. **Resourceful** – having the ability to find clever and quick ways to overcome difficulties
198. **Respectable** – worthy of respect or high esteem
199. **Revolutionary** – extraordinarily good and surprising

Positive Words Starting With the Letter S

200. **Saccharine** – extremely sweet
201. **Sagacious** – acutely wise and insightful
202. **Savvy** – well-informed, perceptive or shrewd
203. **Self-assured** – showing or having confidence and poise
204. **Sensational** – exceptionally good
205. **Sincere** – genuine
206. **Snappy** – energetic
207. **Snazzy** – fashionable
208. **Spellbinding** – fascinating
209. **Splendiferous** – very beautiful
210. **Spunky** – spirited
211. **Stellar** – exceptional
212. **Striking** – sensational or exciting in appearance or in effect

Positive Words Starting With the Letter T

213. **Teeming** – productive
214. **Tender-hearted** – having a great sensibility and kindness
215. **Thoughtful** – demonstrating careful consideration or thought
216. **Thriving** – very profitable and lively

217. **Timeless** – classic and always in style
218. **Tolerant** – tending to accept, allow, permit or understand something or the existence of something
219. **Trailblazing** – innovative
220. **Transcendental** – superior; extraordinary
221. **Tubular** – awesome; cool

Positive Words Starting With The Letter U

222. **Upbeat** – having a fast and positive tone
223. **Uplifting** – inspiring hope or happiness
224. **Upstanding** – respectable
225. **Urbane** – polite

Positive Words Starting With The Letter V

226. **Valiant** – brave and courageous
227. **Vibrant** – lively and bright
228. **Victorious** – being the winner of something
229. **Visionary** – one who has visions or positive ideas about future imprisoned by words
230. **Vivacious** – animated and lively

Positive Words Starting With the Letter W

231. **Warm** – kind and caring
232. **Well-read** – highly educated
233. **Whimsical** – playful and amusing
234. **Whiz-bang** – successful
235. **Wholehearted** – unconditional commitment
236. **Winsome** – charming
237. **Wise** – having knowledge
238. **Witty** – clever and funny
239. **Wizardly** – remarkable in performance, execution or design
240. **Wondrous** – extraordinary
241. **Worldly** – very sophisticated

Positive Words Starting With the Letter X

242. **Xenial** – hospitable to others
243. **Xenodochial** – friendly to strangers or guests

Positive Words Starting With the Letter Y

244. **Yay** – an expression of approval and excitement
245. **Yes** – an affirmative answer or decision
246. **Yummiest** – the most delicious

Positive Words Starting With the Letter Z

247. **Zappy** – energetic and lively
248. **Zazzy** – flashy
249. **Zealful** – passionate enthusiasm
250. **Zealous** – having or exhibiting strong enthusiasm or passion

Exercises you can do at home.

You can use words to change your mood, open your mind, motivate yourself or others. Everything that happens starts with the words we use.

Here are some ideas and strategies that can change your outlook and outcomes

Starting your day.

You can tell a lot about people by the way they start their day. Some of us greet the day with enthusiasm and can't wait to bound out of bed and get started! The rest of us stagger into the bathroom and are shocked to see the person in the mirror, peering back at them. You are either a Morning People or you are not.

If you need to go to work at a specific time, then many of your choices have been made for you by your employer. He dictates what time you get up in order to catch your bus or train. As a result, we stay in bed to the last possible moment, plus five minutes, and spend the rest of the day playing catch up. We start the day running in automatic and going through a daily rituals by habit.

Don't waste anytime thinking, or talking, we don't want to wear our brains out – we might need them later!

No wonder so many people look like zombies on public transport! But does it have to be this way? What if we made different choices? How would that change your day?

There is a big difference to starting your day on purpose, rather than by accident. It is just a different set of choices – ones that could make a dramatic difference. It starts with self-talk. You might as well, nobody else will be speaking to you!

When you first open your eyes. Make a choice to lay there for a second and think grateful thoughts. Think about the good things going to happen today. You have a new day full of new opportunities. New people to meet. Who knows what difference they could make to you? You should now be in the mindset of positive expectation. Now it is time to get up!

Now for your bathroom routine. Positive in negative out! Your biggest asset is waiting for you. The mirror! Coco Channel once said "Beware of mirrors. They only reflect what you think of yourself!" What a great opportunity! Change what you think of yourself!

So when you look in the mirror what do you see? I see the person who has made the choice to get every ounce of value out of the next eight hours.

Every minute is a precious gift and can't be frittered away on non-essentials.

If you work for yourself, you may well be working just a half-day, and it doesn't matter which twelve hours you choose!

The biggest thief of time has to be social media. F.O.M.O is the fear of missing out. Have you counted the number of times you reach into your pocket for your phone to check the news or for the latest post. I challenge you to keep a count during the day. The number might scare you!

To get the most out of each day, be truly present and focused on being in the NOW. Never let a smile be far from your lips. A smile says more about you than you might realise. It tells people how you are feeling and attracts people to you. Apply these principles, and you may be pleasantly surprised at the results!

Jos's List of Encouraging Words

1. This is what you're going through, not who you are.
2. "Believe you can and you're halfway there." —Theodore Roosevelt
3. You are being awesome!
4. This is tough, but you're tougher.
5. Don't stress. You got this!
6. Good luck today! I know you are going to be great.
7. You're making a big change, and I'm so proud of you!
8. Sending some good vibes and happy thoughts your way.
9. "If I cannot do great things, I can do small things in a great way." —Martin Luther King, Jr.
10. I know things are difficult right now, but I also know you've got what it takes to get through it.
11. Sending good thoughts your way—I believe in you and don't doubt for a minute that you will kill it.
12. Keeping you close in my thoughts, today especially.
13. "In the middle of difficulty lies opportunity." —Albert Einstein
14. We've got friends for our happiest days and saddest moments. I hope you know I'm your friend now just as much as ever.
15. I'm so sorry you're going through this, but this too shall pass.
16. You are always on my mind and in my heart.
17. "Courage, dear heart." —C.S. Lewis, *The Chronicles of Narnia Book 3: The Voyage of the Dawn Treader*

18. You are so strong, and you are amazing for facing this with so much courage.
19. If you ever need to talk, or just cry, you know where to find me!
20. I hope you have a better day today.
21. The next chapter of your life is going to be so amazing.
22. "Optimism is the faith that leads to achievement." — Helen Keller
23. I believe in you! And unicorns. But mostly you.
24. What you're going through right now is hard, but I'm rooting for you every minute of every day.
25. I can't wait to catch up with you soon so you can fill me in on all that's been going on in your life.
26. I hope you are surrounded by people who are good for your spirit.
27. You can get through this. Take it from me!
28. Just sending you a quick note to let you know that you're on my mind and in my prayers.
29. It takes serious courage to get on this path and stay on it. Good for you!
30. Remember that you aren't alone as you go through this difficult time. I'm just a phone call away.
31. "It doesn't matter who you are, where you come from. The ability to triumph begins with you. Always." — Oprah Winfrey
32. Be good to yourself. And let others be good to you, too.
33. Take everything one day at a time. I'm just a phone call away.
34. There's no doubt in my mind that you'll succeed in whatever path you choose next.

35. "Be the change that you wish to see in the world." — Mahatma Gandhi
36. Be kind to yourself.
37. You are completely and unconditionally loved.
38. "No matter what you're going through, there's a light at the end of the tunnel." —Demi Lovato
39. Sorry things are crappy. If you need somebody to binge-watch a whole season of something with you, I'm there.
40. You're doing exactly what you should be doing. Hang in there.
41. At a time like this, don't even bother with a dish. Just grab a spoon and start shoveling ice cream straight from the carton.
42. "A champion is defined not by their wins but by how they can recover when they fall." —Serena Williams
43. You're being so strong—and patient. Keep the faith. Things are going to start looking up soon.
44. Thinking of you, and trusting that this difficult time is just a stepping stone along the path to something better.
45. This totally sucks, but you totally don't suck!
46. I'm so sorry you're going through a difficult time. I don't know what to say, except that I care about you, and I'm here for you.
47. Just wanted to send you a smile today.

48. "And you ask, 'What if I fall?' Oh, but my darling, what if you fly?" —Erin Hanson
49. Don't live off of someone else's script. Write your own.
50. Remember, I'm here for you. And I have wine.

51. "You must do the thing you think you cannot do." —Eleanor Roosevelt
52. Stop beating yourself up. You are a work in progress, which means you get there a little at a time, not all at once.
53. "It doesn't matter how slow you go as long as you don't stop." —Confucius
54. A journey starts with one step.
55. "Anything's possible if you've got enough nerve." —J.K. Rowling, *Harry Potter and the Half-Blood Prince*
56. I admire how strong you are!
57. "No matter what people tell you, words and ideas can change the world." —Robin Williams
58. Faith can move mountains. Believe everything is possible and you will change the results!
59. Don't let how you feel make you forget what you deserve.
60. "Try to be a rainbow in someone else's cloud." —Maya Angelou
61. This, too, shall pass. And you are going to look back on this period in your life and be so glad that you never gave up.
62. "It always seems impossible until it is done." —Nelson Mandela

63. "You will never do anything in this world without courage. It is the greatest quality in the mind next to honour." —Aristotle
64. Don't let anyone dull your sparkle.

65. "Always be a first-rate version of yourself, instead of a second-rate version of somebody else." —Judy Garland
66. You are braver than you believe, stronger than you seem, and smarter than you think.
67. "Fall seven times, stand up eight." —Japanese Proverb
68. You're in a storm right now. I'll hold your umbrella.
69. "It is never too late to be what you might have been." —George Eliot
70. Today will never come again. Look forward to tomorrow.
71. "The most beautiful thing you can wear is confidence." —Blake Lively
72. God gave you this life because he knew you were strong enough to live it.
73. "Sometimes when you are in a dark place you think you ave been buried, but actually you have been planted." —Christine Caine
74. You never know how strong you are until being strong is the only choice you have.
75. "The only time you run out of chances is when you stop taking them." —Alexander Pope
76. When the world says, "Give up," hope whispers, "Try it one more time."
77. "Encourage yourself, believe in yourself, and love yourself. Never doubt who you are." —Stephanie Lahart, *Overcoming Life's Obstacles*
78. You have to fight through some bad days to earn the best days of your life.
79. "Trust yourself. You know more than you think you do." —Dr. Benjamin Spock

80. Take a deep breath; it's just a bad day, not a bad life.
81. Every day may not be a good day, but there is something good in every day.
82. "Your life is your message to the world. Make it inspiring." —Sady Ali Khan
83. "When the wrong people leave your life, the right things start happening." —Zig Ziglar
84. You have my full support, no matter what you do.
85. Believe in yourself, because I believe in you!
86. You are in charge of your own happiness.
87. Don't wait for opportunity. Create it!
88. Storms don't last forever!
89. Today's a good day to have a great day.
90. Don't be afraid to try. Be afraid to fail.
91. No one is you and that is your superpower.
92. Don't try to be perfect. Just try to be better than you were yesterday.
93. Don't forget to be awesome.
94. Follow your dreams—they know the way.
95. You are stronger than you think you are.
96. Your attitude determines your direction.
97. A positive mind finds opportunity in everything.
98. It always seems impossible until it's done.
99. Your speed doesn't matter. Forward is forward.
100. Grow through what you go through.
101. Sometimes you win, sometimes you learn.
102. Success doesn't come from what you do occasionally. It comes from what you do consistently.
103. It doesn't matter what others are doing. It matters what you are doing.
104. Mistakes are proof that you are trying.

105. The best view comes after the hardest climb.
106. You are capable of more than you know.
107. If you never try, you'll never know.
108. Every accomplishment starts with the decision to try.
109. I can't wait to see what you do next.
110. Progress, not perfection.
111. It may not be easy, but it will be worth it!
112. You should be so proud of yourself.
113. You can do anything you set your mind to.
114. Don't forget to take notice of how far you have come!
115. Being brave doesn't mean you're not afraid. It just means you try anyway.
116. Make today matter!
117. No matter what happens, you are strong enough to handle it.
118. All things are difficult before they become easy.
119. You don't have to be perfect to be amazing.
120. Tighten your ponytail and try again!
121. Embrace every challenge.
122. Believe in the power of yet.
123 "Don't let your dreams be dreams." —Jack Johnson
124. "The expert at anything was once a beginner." — Helen Hayes
125. Be positive, patient, and persistent.
126. Unless you puke, faint, or die, keep going.
127. "If you're going through hell, keep going." —Winston Churchill
128. Keep going until you are proud.
129. Give yourself some credit for all you've done so far.
130. "The most effective way to do it, is to do it." —Amelia Earhart

131. Tomorrow will worry about itself
132. Every moment is a fresh beginning.
133. You are valuable. Don't let anyone make you believe differently.
134. "Success is getting what you want, happiness is wanting what you get." —Ingrid Bergman
135. Remember why you started.
136. Small progress is still progress.
137. If it was easy, everyone would do it.
138. "Nobody cares if you can't dance well. Just get up and dance. Great dancers are not great because of their technique, they are great because of their passion." —Martha Graham
139. Great things never come from comfort zones.
140. Doing nothing is a great way to change nothing!
141. Nothing will work unless you do.
142. Don't trade your authenticity for approval.

143. "Keep your sunny side up, keep yourself beautiful, and indulge yourself." —Betsey Johnson
144. Remember your why.
145. You can do hard things.
146. Put your hair up in a bun, drink some coffee, and handle it.
147. "We can do no great things, only small things with great love." —Mother Teresa
148. "People, even more than things, have to be restored, renewed, revived, reclaimed, and redeemed. Never throw out anyone." —Audrey Hepburn
149. If you stumble, make it part of the dance.
150. The only time you run out of chances is when you stop taking them.

JOS FREDERIKS

IMPRISONED BY WORDS

www.ingramcontent.com/pod-product-compliance
Lightning Source LLC
Chambersburg PA
CBHW041137110526
44590CB00027B/4050